To

_____

From

_____

Date

_____

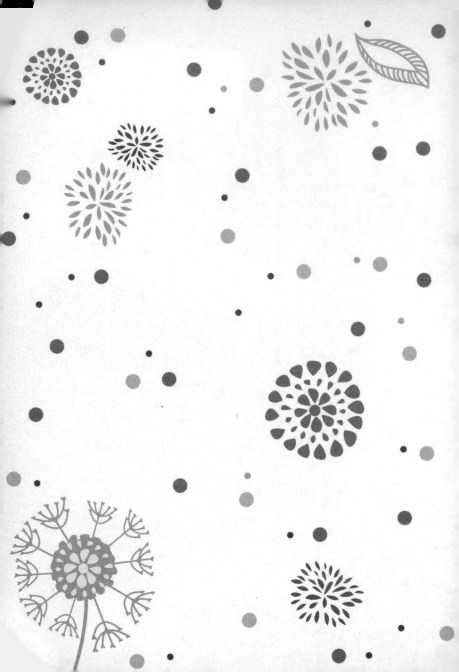

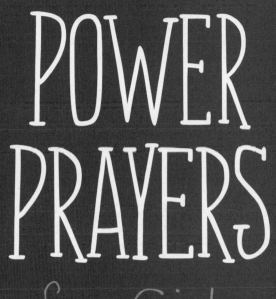

POWER PRAYERS

for Girls

EMILY BIGGERS

SHILOH ! kidz
An Imprint of Barbour Publishing, Inc.

Prayers written by Emily Biggers and Glenn Hascall

Print ISBN 978-1-63058-859-5

eBook Editions:
Adobe Digital Edition (.epub) 978-1-63409-294-4
Kindle and MobiPocket Edition (.prc) 978-1-63409-295-1

Published by Shiloh Kidz, an imprint of Barbour Publishing, Inc., P.O. Box 719, Uhrichsville, Ohio 44683, www.shilohkidz.com.

Our mission is to publish and distribute inspirational products offering exceptional value and biblical encouragement to the masses.

Member of the
Evangelical Christian
Publishers Association

Printed in the United States of America.
05016 0315 DP

CONTENTS

Introduction 7

My Attitude—The Power of My Thoughts 9

My Beauty—The Power of Identity in Christ 19

My Bible—The Power of God's Word 29

My Circumstances—The Power of Perseverance 39

My Dreams—The Power of Expectation 49

My Family—The Power of Love 59

My Fears—The Power of Faith 69

My Friends—The Power of Connection 79

My Future—The Power of Pursuing God's Plan 89

My Gifts—The Power of Service 99

My Habits—The Power of Good Choices 109

My Heart—The Power of a Gentle Spirit 119

My Identity—The Power of Who I Am in Christ 129

My Quiet Times—The Power of Solitude 139

My Salvation—The Power to Rescue My Soul 149

My School—The Power of Education 159

My Strength—The Power of Jesus Christ in Me 169

My Temper—The Power of Self-Control 179

My Time—The Power of Priorities 189

My World—The Power of Compassion 199

My Worry—The Power of Peace 209

Scripture Index 219

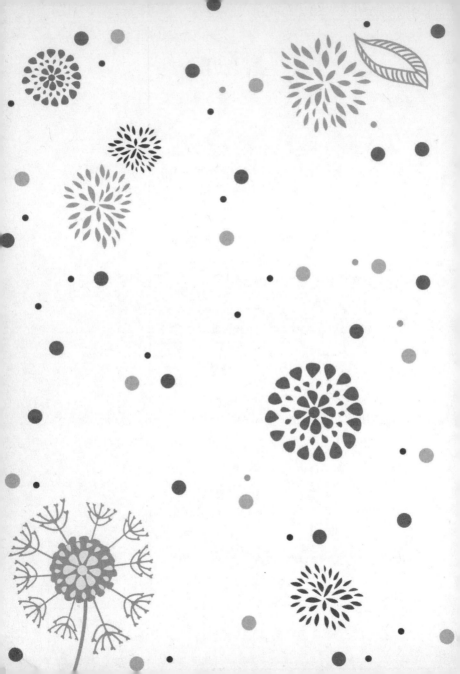

INTRODUCTION

Prayer is communication with God. It is like a conversation. We talk to God and He talks to us. Prayer is a privilege that is available to those who know Jesus. If your heart is open and you are quiet before the Lord, He will speak to you through His Word and through the Holy Spirit. Prayer is the Christian's power source, but sadly, many Christians do not take advantage of it. They go along trying to make it on their own. However, life is not easy. There are hard days. There are decisions to make. Being a light for Jesus in a dark world requires our heavenly Father's help, doesn't it? As a young lady seeking to be more like Jesus each day, you can use this book to help you develop the habit of reading scriptures from the Bible and praying each day. Tap into the power source of prayer. Start today!

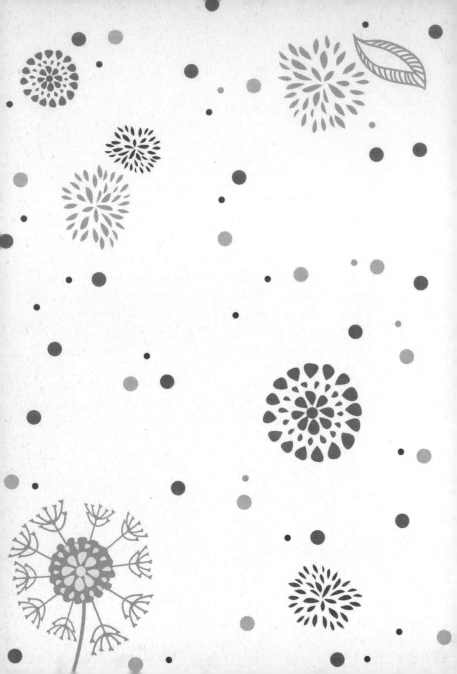

MY ATTITUDE—
THE POWER OF MY THOUGHTS

Often in schools you will see posters that make statements about attitude. They may say things such as "Attitude Is Everything" or "Attitude Is a Small Thing That Make a BIG Difference!" Do you believe this? It is amazing how much of a difference your attitude truly can make. Focusing on the negative and anxiously dwelling on the "what-ifs" of life can make for a really bad day. When you're down, try focusing on God's truth about you. He knit you together in your mother's womb. He has plans for your future that are good, not bad. These truths from the Bible can change your attitude and make for a better day all the way around. Ask God to help you improve your attitude. He is honored when your attitude reflects a thankful heart.

You must have the same attitude that
Christ Jesus had. Though he was God, he did
not think of equality with God as something
to cling to. Instead, he gave up his divine
privileges; he took the humble position of
a slave and was born as a human being.
PHILIPPIANS 2:5–7 NLT

Lord, make me more like Jesus. He was humble and
kind. He didn't flaunt His status as Your Son, but
walked among the people as a teacher and friend.
He led by example. My parents and teachers speak
of being a good leader, leading others in a positive
way. Help me to be that kind of person with an
attitude like Christ's. Help me to love those around
me and to be humble even if I am praised by adults
or friends. Thank You for helping me. Amen.

You were taught to leave your old self—to stop living the evil way you lived before. That old self becomes worse, because people are fooled by the evil things they want to do. But you were taught to be made new in your hearts, to become a new person. That new person is made to be like God—made to be truly good and holy.
EPHESIANS 4:22–24 NCV

Lord, in You I am a new person. I don't have to be my old self. It's so easy to get tangled up in sin, but You free me from my old ways of thinking. Fill my mind with Your goodness and Your ways. Help me to be a new person. Your Word says that I am a new creation in Christ. Help me to live like a new creation, not like a lost soul who is sad and depressed. Put a smile in my heart that I might bring You glory today in my attitude and in my actions. Amen.

May the God who gives endurance and encouragement give you the same attitude of mind toward each other that Christ Jesus had, so that with one mind and one voice you may glorify the God and Father of our Lord Jesus Christ.
ROMANS 15:5–6 NIV

Heavenly Father, I want to include others. I don't want to be the person who divides; instead, I want to be someone who brings people together. Sometimes I get caught up in wanting to hang out with just a certain group of people. I forget about others. At times, I even treat them coldly. Make my attitude more like the attitude Jesus had when He walked on earth. He included. He built unity. He did not divide. I want to have this type of mind-set. Help me, Lord. Amen.

A cheerful heart is good medicine,
but a crushed spirit dries up the bones.
PROVERBS 17:22 NIV

Heavenly Father, I ask today that You would help me to have a cheerful heart. I know that laughter is good medicine. I don't like the taste of most medicines, to be honest, but I know that laughter is sweet! You delight in my laughter because I am Your precious child. You want me to be happy. Even more than a temporary feeling, You want me to have joy deep down in my heart. This kind of joy comes only through Jesus. Thank You for loving me! Amen.

Pride leads to destruction; a proud attitude brings ruin.
PROVERBS 16:18 NCV

Help me, God, to be humble. I know that pride in my heart is not a good thing. Your Word says it brings destruction. I want to be built up in You. I want to build others up also. I don't want destruction in my life. Cause me to see others as important. Help me to remember that everyone around me has a struggle even if I can't see it on the outside. Help my attitude toward others to be kind and loving, not haughty or prideful. Amen.

For the Kingdom of God is not a matter of what we eat
or drink, but of living a life of goodness and peace and joy
in the Holy Spirit. If you serve Christ with this attitude,
you will please God, and others will approve of you, too.
ROMANS 14:17–18 NLT

Lord Jesus, make me a servant. I so often want to be in charge.
Remind me that You are the Lord of my life and that I am to serve
You with joy, peace, and goodness. These attitudes can be found in
me only if I allow the Holy Spirit to influence me. I want to please
You and serve You well. I also want to serve others around me and
help them in any way I can. Amen.

Finally, all of you should be of one mind. Sympathize
with each other. Love each other as brothers and sisters.
Be tenderhearted, and keep a humble attitude.
1 PETER 3:8 NLT

God, sometimes it's hard to remember that other Christians are my
brothers and sisters. Just as I should treat my siblings with love
and care, I should do the same for my brothers and sisters in Christ.
Give me little reminders throughout my day today that we are all
one family. Help me to feel the hurts and see the needs of those
around me. Help me to love as You love—without condition. Amen.

Do everything without complaining and arguing,
so that no one can criticize you. Live clean, innocent
lives as children of God, shining like bright lights in
a world full of crooked and perverse people.
PHILIPPIANS 2:14–15 NLT

Jesus, so many times I am tempted to complain. I
hear others doing it constantly, and I want to join
in on the comments. "I hate homework" or "Why
do I have to empty the trash every single day?" are
words that flow off my tongue before I can even
catch myself. Help me to take every thought to You
before it becomes a complaint. Remind me of all my
blessings, and help me to cut down on the number
of times I complain each day. I know You can help
me to have a better attitude. Thank You, Lord.
Amen.

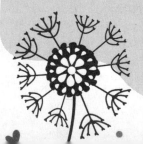

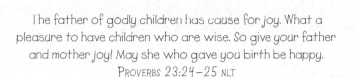

The father of godly children has cause for joy. What a pleasure to have children who are wise. So give your father and mother joy! May she who gave you birth be happy.
PROVERBS 23:24–25 NLT

Heavenly Father, help me to have a good attitude at home. It's easier to act nice when I'm with adults. I know what it means to have good manners. I've been taught to treat adults with respect. When it comes to my own parents, it's harder. I find myself having a bad attitude when they ask me to do things. I want to bring my parents joy. I want to be a godly young person. Help me with this. It's a daily struggle, but I know I can find victory in You! Amen.

"In your anger do not sin": Do not let the sun go down while you are still angry.
EPHESIANS 4:26 NIV

Lord Jesus, I do get angry sometimes. You tell me in Your Word that anger itself is not a sin but that I shouldn't let my anger lead to sin. Please help me to have a good attitude toward others around me even when I'm angry. I don't want to take it out on other people. Give me the self-control I need to keep from sinning when I'm mad. Amen.

Don't use foul or abusive language. Let everything
you say be good and helpful, so that your words will be
an encouragement to those who hear them.
EPHESIANS 4:29 NLT

Dear God, how I want to be an encourager! There are teachers and
friends in my life who encourage me. They build me up with their
words. They make me feel good just by being near me. Make me
more like these people. Jesus was an encourager. He encouraged
and taught His disciples. The Bible says He loved them. Fill my
heart with love for others and put in me a spirit of encouragement.
In Jesus' name, amen.

Don't love money; be satisfied with what you have.
For God has said, "I will never fail you. I will never abandon you."
HEBREWS 13:5 NLT

Heavenly Father, You know my heart. You know all my thoughts—
the good ones and the not-so-good ones. I might as well admit
that I feel jealous at times. I see what someone else has and I want
it. I wish my family had more money. Please remind me that this
attitude is not pleasing to You. Remind me that I have everything
I need in You. I don't want to have a jealous or greedy attitude.
Thank You, Lord. Amen.

My dear brothers and sisters,
always be willing to listen and slow to
speak. Do not become angry easily.
JAMES 1:19 NCV

Dear Lord, make me a good listener. I'm often too
quick to try to talk, talk, talk. People really just want
a listening ear, not a quick fix for their problems.
I know that I feel valued and loved when a family
member or friend listens to me. Give me a kind
attitude toward anyone who comes to me to share
their worries. May I be loving and may I avoid
trying to fill every empty moment with my own
voice. Amen.

For the word of God is alive and active. Sharper than any double-edged sword, it penetrates even to dividing soul and spirit, joints and marrow; it judges the thoughts and attitudes of the heart. Nothing in all creation is hidden from God's sight. Everything is uncovered and laid bare before the eyes of him to whom we must give account.

HEBREWS 4:12–13 NIV

God, I know You see my attitude even when I try to hide it from others. You see my heart and know the way I feel. I want to please You with my thoughts. I want to be able to have a good attitude even when someone treats me wrongly or when I'm disappointed. It's so hard! I can't do it alone, but Your Word says that I can do all things through Christ who gives me strength. Help me to have an attitude today that is pleasing to You. In Jesus' name I pray, amen.

MY BEAUTY—
THE POWER OF IDENTITY IN CHRIST

The world is eager to convince young ladies that their value is found in what they own or wear. The styles change so quickly that it's almost impossible to keep up—and yet girls everywhere are trying! It's very freeing to realize that as a Christian, you don't find your identity in what you look like on the outside. Jesus is not interested in what you wear or how you do your hair or makeup. He sees your heart. We are warned in 1 Timothy against putting too much value on hairstyles and jewelry. The Bible speaks of these things because women have struggled with this issue from the beginning of time. When you are tempted to put too much emphasis on your outward appearance, stop and think about how God sees you. You are a daughter of the King of kings! He cannot love you any more than He already does, and He promises never to love you less.

And I want women to be modest in their appearance.
They should wear decent and appropriate clothing
and not draw attention to themselves by the way
they fix their hair or by wearing gold or pearls
or expensive clothes. For women who claim to be
devoted to God should make themselves attractive
by the good things they do.
1 TIMOTHY 2:9–10 NLT

I like the latest styles, Lord, but I know some are
not appropriate for a Christian girl. Reveal to me
what is okay. Help me to ask myself when I dress
or do my makeup and hair, *Do I look the way You
would like for me to look? Am I trying to draw
attention to myself or am I simply enjoying a new
style?* I want to be modest. It's hard. I need Your
help in this area. Amen.

I praise you because I am fearfully and wonderfully made;
your works are wonderful, I know that full well.
PSALM 139:14 NIV

Thank You, Creator God, for making me. Without You I would not exist. You breathed life into me. You knit me together in my mother's womb. Help me to focus on this when I get down about my appearance. You created me just the way You saw fit. You may have chosen another color of hair or eyes for other girls. But You chose for me to look this way, and I will not criticize myself. In doing that, I'm really cutting You down, God! I don't want to do that. Amen.

But the LORD said to Samuel, "Do not consider his appearance
or his height, for I have rejected him. The Lord does not look
at the things people look at. People look at the outward
appearance, but the Lord looks at the heart."
1 SAMUEL 16:7 NIV

Lord, when You chose a king, You weren't interested in height or appearance. You looked at the heart. When You look at my heart, I pray that You are pleased. Help me to take my attention off what I look like on the outside and pay more attention to working on who I am on the inside. I want to honor You with my thoughts and actions. It's not all about looks! Amen.

> Charm is deceptive, and beauty is fleeting;
> but a woman who fears the Lord is to be praised.
> PROVERBS 31:30 NIV

God, I admit it. I want to be beautiful. I see women and even teens in the movies, and they are so striking. I want different hair than what You gave me. I want to get rid of certain features and have them replaced with prettier ones. I wish I were curvier in some places and smaller in others. God, in Your Word I read that beauty is fleeting. It doesn't last. I want to be known as a young woman who loves the Lord. Help me to want this more than I want a beautiful outward appearance. Amen.

• • • • • • • •

> "Physical training is good, but training for godliness is much better,
> promising benefits in this life and in the life to come."
> 1 TIMOTHY 4:8 NLT

I know that being physically fit is good, but help me to focus on becoming spiritually fit as well. That is what lasts. That is what will benefit me not only in this life but in heaven. I want to grow in my faith through reading Your Word and spending time with You. Help me to find a balance. Help me to dwell on what is most important. Amen.

Even the hairs on your head are counted. So don't be afraid!
You are worth much more than many sparrows.
LUKE 12:7 CEV

God, at school it seems like only the prettiest girls are popular. I don't think that seems right. It's good to know that with You, that is not the case. You love all girls the same. You created us each to be unique and individual. You gave us each special gifts. What we look like on the outside doesn't matter. We are very valuable to You. Thank You for assuring me that my worth doesn't have anything to do with how I look. I love You, Lord. Amen.

A glad heart makes a happy face; a broken heart crushes the spirit.
PROVERBS 15:13 NLT

Dear Lord, I notice people who smile a lot. A smile or a friendly hello can really cheer me up. Please help me to be someone who offers a smile to those around me, whether I know them or not. Make my face a happy one, one that is gentle and accepting even to those who may treat me in an unusual way or act ugly. Sometimes people act that way because they are sad inside. Give me the grace to always wear a smile. Amen.

My servant grew up in the Lord's presence like a tender green shoot, like a root in dry ground. There was nothing beautiful or majestic about his appearance, nothing to attract us to him. He was despised and rejected—a man of sorrows, acquainted with deepest grief. We turned our backs on him and looked the other way. He was despised, and we did not care.

ISAIAH 53:2–3 NLT

Jesus, it helps me to read in the Bible that You were not a strikingly handsome person when You walked this earth. You could have chosen any form. You didn't select a majestic, beautiful one. I think maybe You chose to appear more average because You wanted us to be able to relate to You—just us average people. One day Christians will have new bodies—heavenly bodies. There will be no more sickness. Our bodies will be perfect. I await that glorious transformation when I can be with You in heaven. Amen.

"When you give to someone in need, don't do as the hypocrites do—blowing trumpets in the synagogues and streets to call attention to their acts of charity! I tell you the truth, they have received all the reward they will ever get."
MATTHEW 6:2 NLT

God, outward appearances are so important in this world, but they mean nothing to You. You see the heart behind the surface. Help me to be humble and kind. Help me to give for the sake of giving and not to be seen. There is no reward in making a big deal out of generosity. It's not really generosity at all if I do that. It's a show. I don't want to be showy. I want to be giving. Protect my heart that I might never be tempted to give simply for the outward appearance of it. Amen.

He takes no pleasure in the strength of a horse or in human might. No, the Lord's delight is in those who fear him, those who put their hope in his unfailing love.
PSALM 147:10–11 NLT

It seems like people are always competing, God. They want to be the fastest or the strongest. They want to be the best. I see it in athletics and gym class. While it's fun to compete and good to strengthen our bodies, the most important thing is to love You, Lord, and to shine for You at school. More than being the best, I want to be the one who reaches out to someone who needs a friend. This is what interests You far more than if I win the race or am the most physically fit. Amen.

"It is the same with you. People look at you and think you are good, but on the inside you are full of hypocrisy and evil."
MATTHEW 23:28 NCV

Dear God, people think I am a pretty good girl. They know I go to church and that I'm a Christian. Deep down, there are some ugly thoughts and not-so-nice beliefs in my heart. Will You cleanse me of those? Will You point them out to me? I want to have a pure heart. I don't just want to be seen as "good" because of certain things I don't do or because I attend church. I want my heart to truly honor You in every way. Thank You, Father. Amen.

You should know that your body is a temple for the Holy Spirit who is in you. You have received the Holy Spirit from God. So you do not belong to yourselves, because you were bought by God for a price. So honor God with your bodies.
1 CORINTHIANS 6:19–20 NCV

Heavenly Father, I want to honor You with my body. I know that I am set apart as a Christ follower. There are things I shouldn't do to my body or with my body because they don't honor You. You sent Jesus to die for me that I might have life. Let me honor You with this life, especially with my body. Amen.

Then the Lord God took dust from the ground and formed
a man from it. He breathed the breath of life into
the man's nose, and the man became a living person.
GENESIS 2:7 NCV

God, You made me. That amazes me. You formed man from the
dust. You created human beings with all of the intricate systems of
our bodies and all of our uniqueness. And You did it with nothing
but dust! You breathed into us Your Spirit. Because You made
us in Your image, we are not like any other creature. Human life
is so sacred. Thank You for the knowledge that I am very, very
important to You. I love You, Father. Amen.

You, the source of my life,
showered me with kindness and watched over me.
JOB 10:12 CEV

Lord, You made me and You watch over me every day. You are
not concerned with what I look like. Even on those down-in-the-
dumps days when I'm dressed in an old sweatshirt and jeans, You
shower me with kindness. You love me just as I am. I don't have to
get dressed up or look nice. I don't have to try to be perfect in my
actions. There is nothing I can do to change Your deep love for
me. That's a gift I can't thank You enough for. It feels good to be
loved and accepted. Amen.

Don't be concerned about the outward beauty of fancy hairstyles, expensive jewelry, or beautiful clothes. You should clothe yourselves instead with the beauty that comes from within, the unfading beauty of a gentle and quiet spirit, which is so precious to God.

1 PETER 3:3–4 NLT

What is beauty, God? I think of it as outward, but Your Word says it comes from within. Give me a gentle, loving spirit. Help me to have the type of beauty that does not fade away with years. I am Your child, and I want to be beautiful and precious in Your sight. I know that my focus needs to be on the heart rather than fancy clothes or makeup. Help me, Lord. It's hard not to get caught up in those things when the world says they are so important. Amen.

MY BIBLE—
THE POWER OF GOD'S WORD

The Bible is not like any other book. It is God's holy Word. Every word upon its pages was breathed by God and written down under His direction. The Bible is useful for teaching Christians how to live. It corrects our wrong thinking. It trains us in godliness. In the Bible we learn about doing good deeds in order to glorify our Father in heaven. It can provide great comfort and peace. There are places in the world today where it is against the law to read and study the Bible. People literally hold secret church meetings and risk their lives in order to read the Bible. We should never take for granted our freedom to read God's Word in this country. Honor the Bible. Live by it. Teach it to others. God wants you to take His Word seriously.

"So is my word that goes out from my mouth:
It will not return to me empty, but will
accomplish what I desire and achieve
the purpose for which I sent it."
Isaiah 55:11 NIV

Just like rain makes the grass, trees, and flowers
grow, Your Word goes out and does not return
empty. It is preached in churches and read by
millions. It will serve its purpose. You desire that we
should read Your Word. Many come to know You
through its powerful message of good news. You
want us to learn from Your Word and live according
to it. Your Word is powerful like a double-edged
sword. Every word You speak will serve its purpose.
May I be a listener and a learner. May I take Your
Word seriously that it may accomplish its purpose
in my life. Amen.

Jesus answered, "It is written: 'Man shall not live on bread alone, but on every word that comes from the mouth of God.'"
MATTHEW 4:4 NIV

Jesus, when You were tempted by Satan himself, You told him that the Word of God sustained You. May it nourish my heart and soul just as food nourishes my body. I want to know the Bible so well that when I find myself in tempting spots, I will be able to stand strong against the devil. I love Your Word, God. May I show it through the amount of time I spend reading it versus all the other activities that try to crowd the Bible out of my schedule. Amen.

I will obey your demands, so please don't ever leave me.
PSALM 119:8 NCV

Help me, Lord, to follow Your ways. They are so clear in the Bible. All I need to do is read it and apply it to my life. That's easier said than done. I want to honor You in the way I live. I know I can't keep Your law perfectly and that's why You provided Jesus to die for my sins and make a way for me to be saved. Still, out of my great love for You, I want to live in a way that pleases You. Amen.

Until I come, continue to read the Scriptures to the people, strengthen them, and teach them.
1 Timothy 4:13 NCV

Dear Jesus, I know You're coming back one day. Until then, thank You that I have Your Word. It's here for me to learn from and to share with others. It is a guide for my life. Just like toys and electronics come with users' guides or instruction booklets, You have given me the Bible to live by until You come back for me. Thank You for Your holy Word. Amen.

In the beginning there was the Word. The Word was with God, and the Word was God.
John 1:1 NCV

God, You are eternal and so is Your Word. It will last forever. I cherish the Bible and want to follow Your ways that You teach me on its pages. I know that Your Word is breathed by You and that it is written to teach me and correct me and guide me. Help me to treat it with respect and to memorize its teachings so that I might glorify You in how I live. Amen.

*"I have not departed from the commands of his lips;
I have treasured the words of his mouth
more than my daily bread."*
JOB 23:12 NIV

Lord, I am always hungry. It seems I can't go too long without a meal or a snack! May I be as hungry for Your Word as I am for breakfast, lunch, and dinner. Your Word is greater than my daily bread. Food can only nourish my body, but Your holy scriptures sustain my spirit and my mind. May I stay focused on Your Word and Your ways. Amen.

*"Heaven and earth will pass away,
but my words will never pass away."*
MATTHEW 24:35 NIV

Most things are temporary, God. I don't even have some of the stuffed animals I had a few years ago. Books and special toys I had as a very little girl are long gone. We sell things in garage sales. We throw things away. You tell us in Your Word that even the earth will pass away. One thing that will never pass away is Your Word. May I spend time reading and studying the Bible. It is very important. It is eternal. Amen.

Blessed is the one who does not walk in step with
the wicked or stand in the way that sinners take
or sit in the company of mockers, but whose delight
is in the law of the Lord, and who meditates
on his law day and night.
PSALM 1:1–2 NIV

Dear God, I love to start and finish my day reading
Your Word and meditating on it. Reveal to me the
truths You want me to learn. Guide which verses I
read each day so You might teach me what I need
to know that day. You are all-powerful and can show
me things in Your Word. I trust You to instruct me
as a teacher does a student. I want Your Word to be
the first thing I put into my mind each day and the
last thing I dwell on before I drift off to sleep. Amen.

*"Make them holy by your truth;
teach them your word, which is truth."*
JOHN 17:17 NLT

Lord, it's good to know that the Bible is true. It's not a book of fairy
tales or fantasies. It's a book filled with stories of real men and
women. It tells me about Jesus—when He was born in Bethlehem
and all about His ministry on earth. It is a precious book of truth. I
love Your commands because they keep me safe and they are best
for me. I love Your Word, Father. Amen.

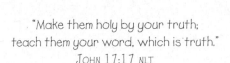

"My sheep listen to my voice; I know them, and they follow me."
JOHN 10:27 NLT

Dear Lord, I like to think of You as my Good Shepherd. I know
Your voice. I'm familiar with it because I read Your Word and I
have Your Holy Spirit living in me and counseling me in Your
ways. Like sheep who know their master's voice even among a
group of shepherds and can pick it out and follow after the right
one, I follow You. May I never turn my ear to another master. I love
You, my Shepherd, and I love Your holy Word. Amen.

"The grass withers and the flowers fall,
but the word of our God endures forever."
ISAIAH 40:8 NIV

Dear God, I cherish the Bible, and I ask You to help me be more serious about reading it daily. I know that it has the secret treasure that I long to find. It is not hidden but available to me on the pages of Your holy Word. I wonder why I put it off so much. I do other things like homework and messing around with electronics. I talk or text with my friends. Then it seems I'm too tired to read the Bible. Help me to make time in the mornings to read Your Word and to pray. Help me to truly cherish Your Word. Amen.

I have taken your words to heart so I would not sin against you.
PSALM 119:11 NCV

God, hide Your Word in my heart so that I can take it with me wherever I go. Write Your ways upon my heart that I might walk in them every single day. I don't want to sin against You. I want to remain pure and I want to be kind and loving. I want to shine the light of Jesus into the world around me. Show me scriptures that will help me most so that I can memorize them and pull them up in my mind when I need them. In Jesus' name I pray, amen.

Everything that was written in the past was written to teach us.
The Scriptures give us patience and encouragement
so that we can have hope.
ROMANS 15:4 NCV

Dear God, Your Word has been around for a long, long time. People were encouraged by it and taught by it many years ago just as we are today. It has stood the test of time, and You declare that it is eternal. It will never pass away. May I become patient and find hope through the reading of Your Word. May I recognize the power of Your Word. In Jesus' name I pray, amen.

Therefore, we never stop thanking God that when you received his message from us, you didn't think of our words as mere human ideas. You accepted what we said as the very word of God—which, of course, it is. And this word continues to work in you who believe.

1 Thessalonians 2:13 nlt

God, Your Word is at work. It draws sinners to repent of sins. It draws hearts to trust in Jesus. Your word is not just made up of human ideas but came straight from You. That's what makes it stand out from all other books. Your word has great power. Help me to tap into the power source of the Bible by committing to read it more regularly. Amen.

MY CIRCUMSTANCES—
THE POWER OF PERSEVERANCE

The apostle Paul truly learned the secret of not letting circumstances determine attitude. He said that he had learned to be content (happy) in all circumstances, whether rich or poor, when well fed but even when hungry. He said that he had learned that he could do all things through Jesus Christ who gave him strength. That same strength source is available to all Christians. There will be mountains and valleys in everyone's life. You will experience highs and lows, good days and bad. There may be some terrible tragedies in your life along with great victories. One thing You can always count on is that Jesus is with You. He will give You the strength to persevere through any situation. Seek Him day after day. He will guide You and love You through the storms of life, and He will be there cheering for You on the good days as well.

Finally, brothers and sisters, whatever is true, whatever is noble, whatever is right, whatever is pure, whatever is lovely, whatever is admirable—if anything is excellent or praiseworthy—think about such things.

PHILIPPIANS 4:8 NIV

I tend to dwell on my circumstances, Lord. I start to convince myself that things will never change and that I am such a loser. Change my negative thoughts into positive ones, Lord. Help me to focus on You and the hope I have as a child of the one true living God. I feel so much better when I read Your Word, when I pray, and when I dwell on all the blessings You have given to me. Amen.

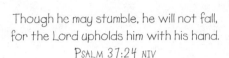

> Though he may stumble, he will not fall,
> for the Lord upholds him with his hand.
> PSALM 37:24 NIV

God, You hold me up with Your righteous right hand. You may allow me to stumble, but You will not let me fall. You have my back. You've got it all under control. All I have to do is hold on to Your hand. Like a parent reaches for a young child's hand to help him or her safely across a busy street, You reach for my hand. You guide me. You carry me. You hold me up. How blessed I am to be a daughter of the King of kings! Amen.

• • • • • • • • •

> Give all your worries and cares to God, for he cares about you.
> 1 PETER 5:7 NLT

God, You have put a lot of great friends in my life. But sometimes I run to everyone and no one seems to have the answer or know what to say to help me. That's because You have put in me a God-shaped hole that can only be filled up by You! Cause me to slow down and rest. I dump my worries at Your feet. You care. You encourage me. You touch my weary forehead. You remind me that You've got my back. Thank You, Lord. Amen.

> Look to the Lord and his strength; seek his face always.
> 1 CHRONICLES 16:11 NIV

Dear God, I seek You in the morning. I seek Your face. I long to walk in the ways You have for me. I want to be in Your will at all times. As the song "Jesus Loves Me" says so clearly: I am weak, but He is strong. You are my source of strength and joy and endurance, Father. Help me never to forget where my help comes from. I will seek You all the days of my life. I know that You are always just a prayer away. Amen.

•　.　•　·　•　.　•　·　•

> With all your heart you must trust the Lord and not your own
> judgment. Always let him lead you, and he will clear
> the road for you to follow.
> PROVERBS 3:5–6 CEV

Lead me, heavenly Father. I will follow. I have tried to go my own way. I have tried striking out on my own and making my own decisions without asking You first. It never goes well! With all of my heart I will trust in You. Your ways are far above my own. You know what is best for me. Make the road clear before me, I pray. Amen.

"Stand firm, and you will win life."
LUKE 21:19 NIV

Dear God, help me to stand firm today. Help me to be a light in the darkness. Help me to shine for You even when I am not in the place I want to be in life. Even when someone else gets what I wanted. . . Even when things seem to be getting worse instead of better. . . Even when I can't understand why You would allow certain things to happen. I want to trust You and I want to stand the test. I love You, Lord. Please grant me strength today. Amen.

Jesus Christ is the same yesterday, today, and forever.
HEBREWS 13:8 NCV

You never change, Lord. Circumstances change. I change. But You remain the same. You are the same yesterday, today, and tomorrow. There will never come a day when I cannot find You or reach out to You. You are always just a prayer away. You promise to never let me go. You promise to guide me with the voice of a good shepherd, a voice I have come to know and trust. Thank You that as my circumstances change and I sometimes feel unstable, I can find an anchor of stability in my Savior. Amen.

The temptations in your life are no different from what others experience. And God is faithful. He will not allow the temptation to be more than you can stand. When you are tempted, he will show you a way out so that you can endure.

1 CORINTHIANS 10:13 NLT

Wow, there are so many temptations all around me, Lord. I try to look the other way. I try to make the right choice. Sometimes I succeed, but often I fail. I give in. I forget to take the thought to Jesus before I act on it. I know this is my lack of faithfulness and not Yours. You are always faithful to give me a way out. Make the way out very clear to me, Father, and give me strength to withstand temptations and to make the right choices. I want to live for You. Amen.

> Blessed is the one who perseveres under trial because,
> having stood the test, that person will receive the crown of life
> that the Lord has promised to those who love him.
> JAMES 1:12 NIV

Lord, this trial seems too hard for me. I know that You promise never to give me more than I can handle. I know You say in Your Word that I can do all things through Christ who gives me strength. I really need an extra measure of strength today. Help me to persevere. Help me to stand strong and to act and speak as I should in the face of this struggle. I want to honor You. Amen.

> And pray in the Spirit on all occasions with all kinds of prayers
> and requests. With this in mind, be alert and always
> keep on praying for all the Lord's people.
> EPHESIANS 6:18 NIV

Jesus, I come to You with my request. I lay it at Your feet. I know You care about even the smallest details in my life. My circumstances don't seem so bad when I compare them to the circumstances of people around the world who may not have their basic needs met today. But I know You understand how big my troubles seem to me. Thank You for caring. Thank You for being there for me to talk to anytime. Prayer is a blessing. Amen.

Be joyful in hope, patient in affliction, faithful in prayer.
ROMANS 12:12 NIV

Heavenly Father, I ask You for joy. Sometimes I get really down and I feel hopeless about my situation. I feel like things will never change and that I'm stuck in a mess. You are my only hope. You tell me to be patient and to keep praying. It's so hard to wait and even harder to believe that my circumstances can change. I will trust in You. Grow my faith that I might truly have hope and joy even in the middle of the storm. Amen.

Let us not become weary in doing good, for at the proper time we will reap a harvest if we do not give up.
GALATIANS 6:9 NIV

Life seems easy for other girls, God. There are girls at school who have great families and who are popular. They make good grades. They always look perfect. It seems like I struggle more than some people. Give me the endurance to keep doing the right thing. I want to follow You when it's easy and when it's hard. I know that I must press on and that it will be worth it. Help me not to compare my circumstances to those of others, and remind me that everyone has their own struggles. Amen.

Rejoice always, pray continually, give thanks in all circumstances;
for this is God's will for you in Christ Jesus.
1 THESSALONIANS 5:16–18 NIV

God, praises flow easily on my good days. I admit that it's hard to praise You when my circumstances are bad. I choose today to give thanks even though things in my life aren't perfect. I know it's Your will for me that I pray to You and even thank You for the trials in my life. I will rejoice in the knowledge that You are still in control. I praise You because You are eternal and all-knowing. You have not left me. Amen.

"I leave you peace; my peace I give you. I do not give it to you as the
world does. So don't let your hearts be troubled or afraid."
JOHN 14:27 NCV

Jesus, thank You for the peace that I can find even in the midst of a very hard time. You give me peace. The world can't give me peace. No matter where I search for it, it just can't be found. There is no person or place or set of circumstances that can give me peace. It has to come from You. Thank You that I know the source of true peace. Calm my troubled heart today. Replace my fear with faith and my anxiety with a calm assurance of Your love. Amen.

We also have joy with our troubles, because we know that these troubles produce patience. And patience produces character, and character produces hope. And this hope will never disappoint us, because God has poured out his love to fill our hearts. He gave us his love through the Holy Spirit, whom God has given to us.
ROMANS 5:3–5 NCV

God, it seems like a lot to ask that I should be joyful in my troubles. I so want to have strong character like the Christian women I look up to. I see how they stand strong and how they love You and serve You, Father. Where does this spiritual maturity come from? I hear them say that they've grown closer to You mostly through their hard times. So, Lord, while I may not jump for joy in this trial, I find hope in You. I ask You to help me face it and grow from it. Amen.

MY DREAMS—
THE POWER OF EXPECTATION

Without dreams, there would be no hope. Perhaps
you dream of being a teacher or a lawyer one day.
Maybe your dream is to have a family. Is there an
instrument you would like to play in the high school
band one day? Do you want to play a certain sport?
Have you considered where God fits in with your
dreams? We cannot see God, but faith is hope in what
we cannot see. We know God is there. We see Him in
His wonderful creation all around us. We sense His
closeness when we pray. God has promised that He
has great plans for you. Pray that your dreams might
fall in line with His will. If there's a dream you've
had for a long time, don't give up. Keep praying and
asking God for whatever it is, but remember that He
may have different plans for you. If so, they will be
even better than your wildest imagination. He is a
good God and He loves to make dreams come true.

The love of money causes all kinds of trouble.
Some people want money so much that they
have given up their faith and caused
themselves a lot of pain.
1 TIMOTHY 6:10 CEV

God, I sometimes count up all of my money and
dream of what I will buy when I have more. I know
this isn't a bad thing for a kid to do really, and yet
I don't want to focus on money. I know that when
I have money, it usually makes me want more. I
spend a lot of time thinking of what I can buy with
it. Help me never to put dreams of money above
You in my life. I don't want to get caught up in
material things. Amen.

> "For I know the plans I have for you," declares the LORD, "
> plans to prosper you and not to harm you,
> plans to give you hope and a future."
> JEREMIAH 29:11 NIV

Dear God, thank You that You already know my future. You tell me in Your Word that You have good plans for me. It's scary sometimes, but I will try to trust that You have it all under control. I have dreams for my future but I believe that You know what's best for me. Please bring about Your will in my life day by day as I walk with You. Please help my desires to match Your will. Amen.

> If you obey the Lord, you will be happy,
> but there is no future for the wicked.
> PROVERBS 10:28 CEV

Heavenly Father, I want to have a good life. I want to walk in Your ways and I want to be happy. I know that true happiness is found only in You. As I make plans for my future and dream big dreams, please help me to always remember that life is only worth living if I am walking with You. I want what You want. I love You, Lord. Amen.

Let all that I am wait quietly before God,
for my hope is in him.
PSALM 62:5 NLT

God, I get in such a hurry. It seems that everything around me
is moving fast. We all want what we want and we want it now.
Right now, in this moment, I rest in You. I sit quietly before You
and take time to remember where my hope comes from. It comes
from the Sovereign God of the universe who made the world and
everything in it. You are my hope. I will wait before You. Amen.

Do not be anxious about anything, but in every situation,
by prayer and petition, with thanksgiving,
present your requests to God.
PHILIPPIANS 4:6 NIV

God, I worry. I admit it. I worry about what people think of me. I
worry about school. I worry about the future stretched out before
me. It's overwhelming. When people ask me what I dream of
being when I grow up, sometimes I think to myself that I'm not
sure I want to grow up! It's scary. Help me to trust You. I bring my
worries about the future to You in prayer. I will take it day by day
as You unfold Your plans for my life. Amen.

> "Ask me and I will tell you remarkable secrets
> you do not know about things to come."
> JEREMIAH 33:3 NLT

Lord, I think I have it all mapped out—what school I'll go to, what I want to be, where I want to live. . . But You know everything. You have amazing secrets that You will reveal to me as I am ready and as I listen to You. Help me to dream big but also to wait on You to reveal Your plans to me. I'm safest when I follow You. Amen.

> Much dreaming and many words are meaningless.
> Therefore fear God.
> ECCLESIASTES 5:7 NIV

God, help me not to daydream so much that I miss today. I catch myself drifting into a fantasy world where things are different or better, where I am happier or in a different set of circumstances. Keep me in the moment. Help me to trust You. I love You, God, and I respect You. I want only what You want for all of my days. Amen.

With all your heart you must trust the Lord and not your own judgment. Always let him lead you, and he will clear the road for you to follow.
PROVERBS 3:5–6 CEV

God, You are trustworthy. You will never lead me astray. You know my heart and all the hopes and dreams it holds. Please help me to find the right paths and chase the right dreams in my life. I want to walk on the paths that will bring glory and honor to Your name. I want to walk on straight and narrow roads rather than following the crowd. I trust You, Father, to lead me in the right direction. Amen.

> I say to myself, "The Lord is my portion;
> therefore I will wait for him."
> LAMENTATIONS 3:24 NIV

Dear God, I get so impatient sometimes. I want all of my dreams to come true now! And yet, I look at Your creation and I am reminded of Your great power. You cause the sun to come up in the morning and to set in the evening. You are in control of my life because I have trusted in Jesus as my Savior. I choose today to wait patiently, asking You to allow my dreams to come true if they are in Your will for my life. Amen.

> "But now, Lord, what do I look for? My hope is in you."
> PSALM 39:7 NIV

Heavenly Father, I don't want to get so caught up in my hopes and dreams that I forget what is most important. I have all I could ever ask for or hope for in my relationship with You. You are before all things, and through You all things were created and hold together. What more could I dream of than the ability to walk and talk with You, God? You are enough for me. Amen.

For you have been my hope, Sovereign LORD,
my confidence since my youth.
PSALM 71:5 NIV

Lord Jesus, I am young still, but I have put my trust in You. I know that no matter what circumstances I am in now or where my dreams may lead me as a teenager and adult, You will be my hope. You are always with me. You never stop loving me no matter what. You make me strong and brave. You walk with me every step of the way. Please help me to remember that You are where I must place my hope and trust. Amen.

There is surely a future hope for you,
and your hope will not be cut off.
PROVERBS 23:18 NIV

God, I long to grow up and be able to do anything I want, and yet I know Your timing is perfect. You knit me together in my mother's womb. You know the number of hairs on my head. The Bible tells me that You have a future for me and that because I follow in Your ways, my hope will never be cut off. Help me to be patient and to know that all of my dreams cannot come true today. I have hope for a very bright future because of You. Amen.

Your heart will be where your treasure is.
LUKE 12:34 NCV

Heavenly Father, it's hard not to dream of having things that I see others enjoying. I see games or electronics that my friends have and I wish I had them, too. I wish for the latest styles in clothing or the newest type of tennis shoes the kids are wearing. May I pause in these moments to think of my true treasure. My true treasure is You. May I never dream of things that are of this world so much that I lose sight of my treasure. Amen.

When doubts filled my mind, your comfort gave me renewed hope and cheer.
PSALM 94:19 NLT

Heavenly Father, sometimes I get down and I can't see beyond my sadness and disappointments. I forget about dreams and goals. I feel depressed. You are my comforter. You are the only One who can bring back my sense of purpose and my happiness. You cheer me up and set me on the right path again, a path of hope and dreams and joy. I love You, Lord. You are so good to me. Amen.

Whether you turn to the right or to the left, you will hear a voice saying, "This is the road! Now follow it."
ISAIAH 30:21 CEV

It's a great comfort to me, God, to know that You are always with me. No matter where I go in life, You are with me. You are pointing the way. You are revealing to me what I should do. If I follow a dream, You will be there guiding me. If I make a mistake or my heart gets broken along the way, You will still be there. Help me to know when to take a risk, when to step out in faith, when to follow my heart. Help me also to know when to make the safer choice. Amen.

MY FAMILY—
THE POWER OF LOVE

Family. It's a powerful word. It makes us think of love and laughter, but it can also bring to mind thoughts of arguments and struggle. Sometimes we fight the most with those we love the most. Sometimes we take our family members for granted. Do you ever stop to think of all that your mom and dad do for you? Do you show love to those in your family, those God has given you as the closest people in your life? When we follow God's plan for loving our family and shine for Him in the midst of even difficult situations, He will bless us. Family is important to God, and He has chosen your family for you. He knit you together in your mother's womb. He knows your name and the number of hairs on your head. He is involved in the details of your life. Whether you live with your birth parents, adoptive parents, one parent, or a guardian, He has chosen the authority figures in your life. He wants you to honor them. Take time to thank Him for the gift of family, and remember that it's important to love your family well.

Love is patient and kind. Love is not jealous, it does not brag, and it is not proud. Love is not rude, is not selfish, and does not get upset with others. Love does not count up wrongs that have been done. Love takes no pleasure in evil but rejoices over the truth. Love patiently accepts all things. It always trusts, always hopes, and always endures.

1 CORINTHIANS 13:4–7 NCV

Lord, I love my family members. Some days it's easy. Other days it's not so easy. Some days I feel like loving them and others days it takes all I've got just to be nice to them. At times, I make bad choices. I'm rude or selfish. I lash out with words that are unkind, words that I know don't please You. Help me to remember that You love me just as much when I'm bad as when I'm good. Help me to love my family every day, no matter what. Amen.

"Honor your father and your mother, so that you may live long in the land the LORD your God is giving you."
EXODUS 20:12 NIV

Dear God, sometimes I find it easy to obey my parents. Other times they seem so unreasonable and they don't understand me at all. I get frustrated and angry. Please remind me in those moments that You have put my parents in a place of authority in my life and You want me to honor them. Give me the ability to hold my tongue. Help me to be calm and to show respect. Amen.

Those who bring trouble on their families inherit the wind. The fool will be a servant to the wise.
PROVERBS 11:29 NLT

Dear heavenly Father, You put me in my family. You decided exactly the family I should be in and You gave each member to me as a gift. No family is perfect, but I do love mine. We have good days and bad days, joys and sorrows, fun times and bad arguments. Help me to shine Your light into my family. Help me to bring them only good, never harm. May I forgive quickly and love strongly. Amen.

"As for me and my family, we will serve the LORD."
JOSHUA 24:15 NCV

Lord, I look around me and I see all kinds of people. I see all kinds of families making all kinds of choices about what is important. Some make sports their god. Others worship TV shows or travel. I want to serve You. I want You to be the most important part of my life, and I would love it if my whole family felt the same way. If we put You first in everything we do, I know that the rest will fall into place as it should. Amen.

My child, listen when your father corrects you.
Don't neglect your mother's instruction.
PROVERBS 1:8 NLT

God, I'm getting a little older and sometimes I just want to do things my way. It's hard always having to listen to my parents tell me what to do when and how to do it. Give me a heart that tries to understand they love me. Help me to realize that usually they really do know best. They've been living longer than me, and I know they have my best interests at heart. Help me to treat my parents as I should. Amen.

> To discipline a child produces wisdom,
> but a mother is disgraced by an undisciplined child.
> PROVERBS 29:15 NLT

Lord, I get so upset when I'm grounded or punished by my parents. I feel frustrated and I don't like the feeling that I have disappointed them. I realize that one of the reasons You have put my parents in my life is to discipline me. Discipline is never fun, but I know You say in Your Word it is necessary. Give me the grace to accept my parents' decisions, and help me to learn from my mistakes and from the consequences. Amen.

> Therefore, whenever we have the opportunity, we should do good
> to everyone—especially to those in the family of faith.
> GALATIANS 6:10 NLT

Lord, remind me that every believer in Christ is part of my family. They are my brothers and sisters through You. Put before me opportunities to show love to other Christians. Whether it's helping an elderly person or someone younger than me, give me a heart of love. Help me to see and grasp chances to brighten others' days and to help them in any way I can. I know this is important. Amen.

Children, obey your parents in the Lord, for this is right. "Honor your father and mother"—which is the first commandment with a promise—"so that it may go well with you and that you may enjoy long life on the earth."

EPHESIANS 6:1–4 NIV

Heavenly Father, thank You for my parents and for their authority in my life. I want to go my own way, do my own thing, and find my own way in the world. But I know they've been put over me in order to help me. I will obey them. Unless they direct me to do something that goes against Your Word, I will always choose obedience. Give me a heart of submission that honors those in authority in my life. I know You want this of me. Amen.

God decided in advance to adopt us into his own family
by bringing us to himself through Jesus Christ. This is what
he wanted to do, and it gave him great pleasure.
EPHESIANS 1:5 NLT

Dear God, thank You for bringing me into Your family through
Jesus Christ. Thank You for choosing to adopt me as Your own
child. You didn't have to do that. You wanted to. You wanted me
as Your little sheep, Good Shepherd. You selected me. Thank You,
God. It feels good to know the voice of my Shepherd will always
direct my paths. It feels good to belong with You. You are my
safety and my joy. I love You, Lord. Amen.

"The second command is this: 'Love your neighbor as you love
yourself.' There are no commands more important than these."
MARK 12:31 NCV

God, love shows up again and again in the Bible. It must be
important to You. It must be powerful. I know it is. You tell me
to love my neighbor as myself. When I stop to think about it,
my neighbors are all those around me. They include my family,
classmates, teachers, friends, and teammates. Help me this day to
find little ways to show great love to those around me, even those
who live under the same roof with me! Amen.

Those who have been born into God's family do not make a practice
of sinning, because God's life is in them. So they can't keep
on sinning, because they are children of God.
1 JOHN 3:9 NLT

God, thank You for sending Jesus to die for my sins, making a way
for me to be part of Your family. No earthly father is perfect, but
You are my heavenly Father and You are above all things. Your
ways are wise, and in Your perfection, You make no mistakes.
You have chosen my earthly family and planted me in it. Give me
grace to love my family well. I am so blessed to be a child of the
living God, and I am also blessed to have a family where I belong
and matter. Amen.

You, your children, and your grandchildren must respect the LORD
your God as long as you live. Obey all his rules and commands
I give you so that you will live a long time.
DEUTERONOMY 6:2 NCV

Dear heavenly Father, some people have a heritage of a family
that loves and serves You. Others are the first in their families to
follow Jesus. Either way, You promise blessing to those who follow
You and who lead their families in Your ways. Help me to stand
out as a believer and help my family to be blessed through my
faithfulness to You. I want You to always be honored as the King
of kings and Lord of lords in my family. Amen.

Jacob was the father of Joseph. Joseph was the husband of Mary,
and Mary was the mother of Jesus. Jesus is called the Christ.
MATTHEW 1:16 NCV

Jesus, You had an earthly family. You grew up with a mom and
dad and siblings. Even though God was Your Father, You worked
with Your earthly father in his wood shop. You learned from him
how to be a good carpenter. The Bible says Your mother was a
woman who cherished things in her heart. She sounds like a loving
person. Help me to honor my parents as You honored Yours. It's
not always easy, Jesus. Amen.

She had a sister called Mary, who sat at the Lord's feet listening
to what he said. But Martha was distracted by all the preparations
that had to be made. She came to him and asked, "Lord, don't you
care that my sister has left me to do the work by myself? Tell her
to help me!" "Martha, Martha," the Lord answered, "you are worried
and upset about many things, but few things are needed—
or indeed only one. Mary has chosen what is better,
and it will not be taken away from her."
LUKE 10:39–42 NIV

Jesus, I find myself not much different from Martha sometimes. I
want to tell on my siblings for doing things I think they shouldn't.
I could learn a lot from Mary, the sister who sat at Your feet and
listened to Your teachings. I'm a busybody at times. Help me to
slow down and listen for Your still, small voice. And help me to
realize that my siblings may be different from me. You gave us
all different personalities and gifts. Help me not to judge or boss
them. Let me leave that to You! Amen.

MY FEARS—
THE POWER OF FAITH

Jesus came that we might be saved by grace through faith in His death on the cross for our sins. He rose again three days later and appeared to many. Then He ascended into heaven where He sits at God's right hand. He will come again to gather His children. If you have placed your faith in Christ, you have eternal life to look forward to. Actually, it has already begun in the abundant life available to you on earth. It all starts with faith. No one can make the decision to follow Jesus for you. It is a personal choice. It is believing in Someone you cannot see before you but in whom you trust just the same. There is great power in faith. It will carry you through your darkest days and encourage others as they wonder how you can face such trials without being shaken in your love for Jesus. Ask God to build up your faith. According to the Bible, there is great power even in faith the size of a tiny seed.

But you, dear friends, by building yourselves up in your most holy
faith and praying in the Holy Spirit, keep yourselves in God's love
as you wait for the mercy of our Lord Jesus Christ
to bring you to eternal life.
JUDE 1:20–21 NIV

Dear Jesus, so many things tear me down in this world. My faith
builds me up instead. When I spend time in Your Word and in
prayer each day, I find great strength. I feel prepared to face
the day no matter what is thrown at me. I am learning that faith
requires waiting. I must wait on Your will and Your plans for
my life to unfold. I must wait on Your second coming. It will be
glorious! I love You, Lord. Amen.

Let love and faithfulness never leave you; bind them around
your neck, write them on the tablet of your heart.
PROVERBS 3:3 NIV

God, I love that my faith can go with me wherever I go. If I'm at
school, I can whisper a prayer to You as I walk down a hallway or
begin to take a hard exam. If I'm out with my friends, I can lean on
my faith to help me face temptations, whether it be in the area of
gossip or taking part in other things I know are not of You. May I be
found faithful to You in every situation. In Jesus' name I pray, amen.

Jesus said to the woman,
"Your faith has saved you; go in peace."
LUKE 7:50 NIV

God, I read about Your miracles. So many times You mention the person's faith. Faith must be important to You. You tell us in Your Word that even if we have faith the size of a mustard seed, it is enough to move mountains. I want to have that kind of faith, Lord. Some days I don't think mine is even as big as that tiny seed. Give me faith that grows with each passing day. I love You, Lord. Amen.

So that your faith might not rest on human wisdom,
but on God's power.
1 CORINTHIANS 2:5 NIV

Lord, sometimes I try to figure it all out. My future. My worries. Then I usually come around to remembering that my faith must be in You, not in my own weak ways and abilities. I can't understand things or fix them, but You can. You are all-powerful, all-knowing, and You care about the circumstances of my life. I choose to place my faith in Your power and not my own today. Amen.

Because of Christ and our faith in him, we can now come
boldly and confidently into God's presence.
EPHESIANS 3:12 NLT

I am not confident in and of myself, God. I find myself frightened
when kids at school say mean things to me or call me names. I
begin to believe them sometimes. I know that Jesus died for me.
I truly do have faith. Help me to be bolder and more confident at
school. Remind me that You are always with me and that through
my faith in Christ, I have a mighty God at my side day in and day
out. Amen.

Be on your guard; stand firm in the faith;
be courageous; be strong.
1 CORINTHIANS 16:13 NIV

God, I find great strength in my faith. When others ask me why I
won't do something that I know goes against Your Word, I lean on
my faith. I am strong and bold in You because I trust You to back
me up when I'm in a corner. When I'm tempted, I have the ability
to stand firm against the devil's tricks. I lean on my faith. Thank
You, Father, for helping me to have faith. Strengthen and grow my
faith so that it becomes even greater, I ask. Amen.

In the same way, faith by itself,
if it is not accompanied by action, is dead.
JAMES 2:17 NIV

Lord, help me to stand out as different from nonbelievers who don't place their faith in You. May my actions and my words cause others to wonder why I do and say the things I do. May my good works point lost people to faith in You. Faith without works is dead. That's a strong statement. May my works glorify You and honor You. I want to live out my faith in my school, my neighborhood, and everywhere I go. In Jesus' name I pray, amen.

So in Christ Jesus you are all children of God through faith.
GALATIANS 3:26 NIV

What a blessing to be called a child of the living God. It is not through anything I have done or ever will do that I am saved. I am saved by grace, through my faith in Jesus. It's Jesus who makes the way for me to come before You even now and know that You hear my prayers. Faith is the bridge that I can cross in order to stand before You. Thank You for faith in Christ that gives me eternal hope and joy. Amen.

I have been crucified with Christ and I no longer live,
but Christ lives in me. The life I now live in the body, I live by faith
in the Son of God, who loved me and gave himself for me.
GALATIANS 2:20 NIV

Jesus, living by faith is so freeing. I don't have to try to get everything right. And I'm not just living for the day or for worldly pleasures. The things that are important in this world are so unimportant in Your kingdom. Material wealth is nothing. Popularity is nothing. Give me the strength to resist the urge to look back at my sinful nature. It's always there, but You are stronger. Increase my faith, I pray. Amen.

Now faith is confidence in what we hope for
and assurance about what we do not see.
HEBREWS 11:1 NIV

Dear God, sometimes I feel really beat down. There are bullies at school who act ugly. They can make people feel really bad about themselves. I'm thankful that I have confidence through You that You are with me. I know that I matter to You and that You see me as Your precious child, not the way the bullies define me. I know that things will get better. I have to face my fears and trust that a brighter day is coming. I find a calm assurance in being Your child. Amen.

*When we get together, I want to encourage you in your faith,
but I also want to be encouraged by yours.*
ROMANS 1:12 NLT

Make me an encourager, Lord. When I'm with other believers,
help me not to just soak it up but also to give. I am so encouraged
when I hear others' stories. Make me aware that my own testimony
is powerful as well. I want to encourage others to stand strong in
their faith. Give me opportunities to do just that, and give me the
boldness to share what You are doing in my life so that I can boast
in Your glory! Amen.

*We are made right with God by placing our faith in Jesus Christ.
And this is true for everyone who believes,
no matter who we are.*
ROMANS 3:22 NLT

Dear heavenly Father, sometimes I feel like I've messed up one
too many times. I feel like I can't come to You again and apologize
and ask You to "take me back." This is just a feeling. It is not truth.
The truth is that I am not made right with You through my actions.
I am made right with You through Jesus. Forgive my sins this day,
Lord. And remind me that I can always come before You in faith.
No matter what. Amen.

But people are counted as righteous, not because of their work,
but because of their faith in God who forgives sinners.
ROMANS 4:5 NLT

God, You are so faithful to me. You never waver the way that I
do. I'm glad I serve a faithful God. I know that I am not counted
righteous because of what I do. I know it comes only through the
free gift of salvation. I do want to please You, though, Lord. I want
to live out my faith. Thank You for showing Yourself faithful in my
life on the good days and the bad alike. Make me faithful as well. I
will never be perfect, but I can grow in my faith. Amen.

Because of our faith, Christ has brought us into this place of
undeserved privilege where we now stand, and we confidently
and joyfully look forward to sharing God's glory.
ROMANS 5:2 NLT

Jesus, I don't deserve the privilege of sharing in God's glory. It is
undeserved. Like a Christmas or birthday gift or like a debt paid off
by another who owed nothing but took on the great debt I owed,
You have given me the free gift of salvation and forgiveness of my
sins. Abundant life now and eternal life in heaven with You when
I die. . .I humbly thank You for the gift. I place my faith in You this
day and walk with You, my Savior. Amen.

He guards the paths of the just and protects those
who are faithful to him.
PROVERBS 2:8 NLT

God, Your protection is so apparent in my life. I feel it. I sense it.
You lay out the way that I should go, and if I'm paying attention,
I see it and follow in it. Help me to always remain faithful to
You. When I stray, I sometimes wind up on a road that leads to
nowhere. Protect my heart and mind, Lord, from the ways of the
world. I want to faithfully follow You. In Jesus' name I pray, amen.

So we fix our eyes not on what is seen, but on what is unseen,
since what is seen is temporary, but what is unseen is eternal.
2 CORINTHIANS 4:18 NIV

Lord, I like proof. I look for it. I like to hold things in my hand. I
like to see how they work. Faith is not like that. It's not something
I can see, but it is very real nonetheless. I look around me and
realize that most of what I see is temporary. You are eternal. I will
choose to fix my eyes on Jesus. When I do, the world becomes dim
in the light of His amazing grace. Amen.

The disciples went and woke him, saying, "Master, Master, we're going to drown!" He got up and rebuked the wind and the raging waters; the storm subsided, and all was calm. "Where is your faith?" he asked his disciples. In fear and amazement they asked one another, "Who is this? He commands even the winds and the water, and they obey him."
LUKE 8:24–25 NIV

Jesus, I almost want to laugh at the disciples—or scold them. It seems so crazy to me that they would fear drowning when You were aboard their boat! Didn't they know that You were God? The storms and the waves have nothing on the Master of the universe! But I probably would have been the same as they were, calling out to You in worry. I don't trust You with my circumstances sometimes. I get worried even though I know You are right here with me. Give me great faith, Lord. I want to trust You more. Amen.

MY FRIENDS—
THE POWER OF CONNECTION

Friends are the family we get to pick! It is so important to choose your friends carefully. God desires for His children to connect with other Christians. You need the support of others who view the world the way you do. Nonbelievers don't make decisions in the same way that believers do. This is not to say that Christian friends are perfect or will never steer you in the wrong direction or let you down. But those who are truly following God are more likely to be solid friends and give godly advice when you ask for it. There is great strength to be found in a true friend. It takes being a good friend to have a good friend, so ask God to make you a good friend to others and, likewise, to bless you with good friends.

"And if you are nice only to your friends, you are no better than other people. Even those who don't know God are nice to their friends."
MATTHEW 5:47 NCV

Heavenly Father, give me an opportunity today to be kind to someone who needs a smile or a word of encouragement. When I stick only in my little group of friends, I'm not acting like Jesus did when He walked this earth. He noticed people around Him who were sick or lonely. He spoke to them. I remember the story of Jesus going to Zacchaeus's home. Zacchaeus was someone who really needed a friend. Jesus changed his life by being that friend to him. Make me more like Jesus. Amen.

> "Why do you notice the little piece of dust in your friend's eye,
> but you don't notice the big piece of wood in your own eye?"
> MATTHEW 7:3 NCV

God, I am so quick to judge my friends and to point out what they are doing wrong. When I look closely at my own life, I see just as many areas where I need to change and grow. Help me to be more tolerant of others' weaknesses. I should work to become a better friend myself rather than finding fault in others. Soften my heart and help me to see the good in my friends rather than the bad. In Jesus' name I pray, amen.

> While we were God's enemies, he made us his friends through
> the death of his Son. Surely, now that we are his friends,
> he will save us through his Son's life.
> ROMANS 5:10 NCV

God, You are my truest friend. You sought me out and saved me even though I was a sinner. I am truly saved by Your grace through Jesus, and I am so thankful for that. It's amazing to think that through Jesus' blood shed on the cross, my sins are forgiven and I can be a friend of the God of the universe. Thank You for being my very best friend. You are always there. I love You, Lord. Amen.

A troublemaker plants seeds of strife;
gossip separates the best of friends.
PROVERBS 16:28 NLT

Gossip is tempting, God. I don't want to be one who spreads
rumors or shares secrets only for the sake of stirring up problems.
I pray that You will stop me just in time when I'm about to share a
juicy bit of news or something that is not necessary to tell others.
Help me to be very careful what I say. I know it's impossible to get
the words back once they are spoken. You tell me in Your Word
that the tongue can be used for good or for bad. Help me to build
my friends up with my words and never tear them down. Amen.

Love prospers when a fault is forgiven,
but dwelling on it separates close friends.
PROVERBS 17:9 NLT

Heavenly Father, You are quick to forgive me, and yet sometimes
I find it so hard to forgive others. Make me more forgiving.
Remind me of my many sins and the great price You paid for
them. You watched Your only Son die on a cross in order that
my sins might be forgiven. I have no right to hold grudges or to
be angry with others. Help me to be quick to forgive my friends
when they wrong me. Amen.

There are "friends" who destroy each other,
but a real friend sticks closer than a brother.
PROVERBS 18:24 NLT

Give me discernment, God, that can tell the difference between
true friends and those who are not so true. There are all kinds of
people in this world. Some people are only out for "number one."
They will quickly turn on a friend. Give me loyal friends, I pray.
I need friends who will be there through the good and the bad. I
thank You for those few close friends in my life who stick closer
than brothers or sisters. Amen.

Wounds from a sincere friend are better
than many kisses from an enemy.
PROVERBS 27:6 NLT

God, I've heard that it's good to speak the truth in love. Sometimes
when a friend tells me the truth, it hurts. It stings. I think it's because
I know they are right! Give me a heart that accepts constructive
criticism from friends. Give me wisdom to know when I need to
change based on what a friend shares with me. It may not always be
what I want to hear, but it is for my own good. Amen.

Even my best friend, the one I trusted completely, the one who shared my food, has turned against me.
PSALM 41:9 NLT

People mess up, Lord. They hurt us. They are only human. When a friend turns against me, it really hurts. Give me grace with those people who hurt me. I know I have hurt others also. Forgive me for times when I haven't been a true friend. God, I know You are the only One who will never let me down. I choose to place my trust in You. Help me to be faithful to You. You are so faithful to me no matter what. You are not like us, God. Your friendship never fails. Amen.

As iron sharpens iron, so a friend sharpens a friend.
PROVERBS 27:17 NLT

Thank You, God, for Christian friends. Thank You for friends who come alongside me and make me a better person. Thank You for friends who encourage me to spend time in Your Word and to go to church where I can be around other Christians. I need friends like that. Please continue to provide Christian friends for me and help me to be a good friend to others in my life. Amen.

Young people who obey the law are wise; those with wild friends bring shame to their parents.
PROVERBS 28:7 NLT

Dear God, I need Your help. I haven't always been wise in picking my friends. Friends have a lot of power in my life. They can lead me in the right or the wrong direction. I want to have friends who are cool and popular, but sometimes those people are not the type of friends I need. They lead me down paths that are not pleasing to You to do things that my parents don't allow me to do. Give me discernment as I seek to choose friends who love and follow Your ways. Amen.

The sweet smell of incense can make you feel good,
but true friendship is better still.
PROVERBS 27:9 CEV

Heavenly Father, there is not much better than a good friend. I enjoy laughing and hanging out with my good friends. They lift my spirits. They make me forget my troubles and worries. Friends are a true blessing in my life. Thank You for providing good friends. I pray that I will always be a good friend to others. Help me to reach out to someone who needs a friend today. Amen.

I am a friend to anyone who fears you—
anyone who obeys your commandments.
PSALM 119:63 NLT

Lord, it's amazing how I can visit another church—even one far from home—and still feel comfortable. I find family there. Christ followers are my brothers and sisters. I have a lot in common with anyone who calls Jesus their Lord and Savior. Even if we are different ages or from different backgrounds or cultures, we have the most important thing in common—You! Amen.

And Jonathan had David reaffirm his oath out of love for him,
because he loved him as he loved himself.
1 SAMUEL 20:17 NIV

God, David and Jonathan were friends who stuck closer than brothers. When I read about Jonathan loving David as himself, it challenges me. Do I love my friends that way? Would I literally do anything for a friend? Am I quick to run when things get tough, or do I stick it out and remain true to my friends? I want to be a good friend. Show me the way to do this, I ask. Amen.

* * *

The disciple Jesus loved was sitting next to Jesus at the table.
JOHN 13:23 NLT

Jesus, even You had "levels" of friends. You were a friend to all You met. You loved the world enough to die for all of us! But You had Your twelve closest friends, those who walked and talked with You—the ones we know as Your disciples. Even among the twelve, the Bible tells us there was "one You loved." It shows me that it's okay to have one friend who is closer than the rest. I pray that I will always have a close friend in my life. I pray that I will always be one to someone else as well. Amen.

A friend loves you all the time,
and a brother helps in time of trouble.
PROVERBS 17:17 NCV

God, I have a lot of friends who are just friends at school or friends on a sports team. They are fun to hang out with, but I wouldn't share my deepest worries or struggles with them. Then there are those few friends You have put in my life who I can tell anything to. They are there when the sun is shining, but they also remain true when I'm really down in the dumps. They "get it." They pray for me. They encourage me. They are solid and true friends. Thank You for the friends who love me all the time. In Jesus' name I pray, amen.

MY FUTURE—
THE POWER OF PURSUING GOD'S PLAN

The future can seem overwhelming. It looms before you. You try to stretch your mind to imagine it, and yet you always fail. It is impossible for a human being to see the future. But what is impossible for man is possible for God. God is omniscient, or all knowing. He knows everything past, present, and future. He is in complete control of the universe. If you woke up this morning, He ordained it. This means He decided it would be good for you to live another day, take more breaths, and have more opportunities to shine as a light for Him in this world. Trust the Lord with the future. It is best when it's left in His hands. He is big enough to handle your today and all of your tomorrows. Ask God each day to help you to trust Him and to follow Him. He will lead you into a bright future that He planned for you before you were born!

Does a fig tree produce olives, or a grapevine produce figs? No, and you can't draw fresh water from a salty spring. If you are wise and understand God's ways, prove it by living an honorable life, doing good works with the humility that comes from wisdom.

JAMES 3:12–13 NLT

Dear God, I just want to honor You every day of my life. As people look at me both today and in the future, please let them see the light of Jesus in my life. No matter where You take me, no matter what career I have or where I live, I want to do good works and love others. I want to be humble and walk with You. I don't know where I will be next year, much less when I'm a grown-up. But I want to keep walking with You. Amen.

"For I know the plans I have for you," declares the LORD,
"plans to prosper you and not to harm you,
plans to give you hope and a future."
JEREMIAH 29:11 NIV

The future seems really big, God. It hangs around out there in front of me, and yet I cannot see it or touch it. I can set goals and make plans, but I really have no idea what direction my life will take. I have to trust You. That's not easy for me. I like to be in control! As I face this day, give me the strength to surrender to Your plans for my life. Help me to enjoy this day and use it for Your glory, God. Help me to trust You with the days ahead. Amen.

What happens now has happened in the past,
and what will happen in the future has happened before.
God makes the same things happen again and again.
ECCLESIASTES 3:15 NCV

Heavenly Father, You are a God of order and patterns. You are consistent. You are constant, never changing. Just as You walked with Christ followers of past generations, You walk with us today. You will lead me just as You led those who came before me. You put Noah and his family on an ark to preserve their lives. You protected David from bears and even from a giant. I will trust that You will lead and protect me as well. Amen.

He is before all things, and in him all things hold together.
COLOSSIANS 1:17 NIV

God, I've heard stories of crystal balls and fortune tellers. Certainly I don't believe in such things, and I stay away from them! I have to admit, though, that it would sometimes be nice to know where I'm headed. The future is such a mystery, Father. Give me confidence to face life day by day, aware that I may not know the future but I know the One who holds it in His hands. In Jesus' name I pray, amen.

And we know that God causes everything to work together for the good of those who love God and are called according to his purpose for them.
ROMANS 8:28 NLT

Where will I go and what will I do in the future, Lord? It's hard to live day by day not knowing these things. I'm afraid I will make a mistake. I'm afraid I will mess up Your will and Your plan for my life. Scriptures can really comfort me when I begin to worry about this. You remind me with Your still, small voice that You are in control. You will use even my mess-ups for good. Amen.

God makes everything happen at the right time. Yet none of us can ever fully understand all he has done, and he puts questions in our minds about the past and the future.
ECCLESIASTES 3:11 CEV

Dear Lord, I have questions about the past and the future. I guess it's just how we are put together as humans. We wonder about what has been and about what is going to be. You are a good God. You are sovereign. You make everything happen at the right time. Even when I don't understand Your timing, it is perfect. I choose to trust You and Your perfect timing in my life. Amen.

"For my thoughts are not your thoughts, neither are your ways my ways," declares the LORD. "As the heavens are higher than the earth, so are my ways higher than your ways and my thoughts than your thoughts."
ISAIAH 55:8–9 NIV

God, I have thoughts and plans, but You tell me in Your Word that Your thoughts and plans are higher than mine. It's good to know that someone wiser and bigger than me has great plans for me. Help me to listen to Your still, small voice. Help me to walk in Your ways and be guided by Your hand always. Even today. Amen.

"He said, 'The God of our ancestors chose you long ago to know his plan, to see the Righteous One, and to hear words from him. You will be his witness to all people, telling them about what you have seen and heard. Now, why wait any longer? Get up, be baptized, and wash your sins away, trusting in him to save you.' "

ACTS 22:14–16 NCV

You know what You're doing, don't You, God? You knew when Saul was a young boy growing up in a Jewish household that You would change the direction of his life. On a road to Damascus, on his way to kill Christians, You would shine a bright light and blind that man. You would alter his plans greatly! You made him into the greatest preacher of the Gospel who ever lived. Help me to be open to a direction change. I want to follow hard after You no matter where You lead me or how You choose to use me, Lord. Amen.

94

The LORD knows all human plans; he knows that they are futile.
PSALM 94:11 NIV

Heavenly Father, I can worry and stress about the future, or I can realize that You have it all under control. You are the Creator. You keep the earth turning on its axis. You know each of Your children by name. You never sleep. You are always watching over us. My plans mean nothing compared to Yours. I know that You are good and that You have good plans for me. Thank You, Lord. Amen.

The LORD will work out his plans for my life— for your faithful love,
O LORD, endures forever. Don't abandon me, for you made me.
PSALM 138:8 NLT

God, everyone is always asking me what I want to be when I grow up, and honestly, I have no clue. I mean, I have some ideas. . .but sometimes all the choices seem overwhelming. Help it to be enough that I am choosing to follow You with all my heart. You are faithful even when I stray from You or begin to make my own plans and follow my own desires. You never leave me. I trust You to work out Your plans for my life. Amen.

They asked, "Who healed you? What happened?" He told them,
"The man they call Jesus made mud and spread it over my eyes
and told me, 'Go to the pool of Siloam and wash yourself.'
So I went and washed, and now I can see!"
JOHN 9:10–11 NLT

You can change my future in a moment, Lord. You are a difference
maker. You are a game changer. Just as You gave sight to the blind
and healed others of the horrible disease called leprosy, You can
change my current circumstances. Nothing is impossible with
You, God. Take the rough things in my life and change them if
You see fit. Use them to strengthen my character. Bring about the
future that You have planned for me, I pray. Amen.

Then the LORD said to Abraham, "Why did Sarah laugh? Why did she
say, 'I am too old to have a baby'? Is anything too hard for
the LORD? No! I will return to you at the right time
a year from now, and Sarah will have a son."
GENESIS 18:13–14 NCV

God, nothing is too hard for You. Nothing is impossible for a God
big enough to create the whole world! Even when things seem
impossible, they are not. You proved this when You allowed Sarah
and Abraham to have a baby in their old age. It seemed so crazy that
Sarah laughed when she heard the idea. But it happened. Help me to
believe in the impossible because I have a great big God. Amen.

She is strong and is respected by the people.
She looks forward to the future with joy.
PROVERBS 31:25 NCV

It's wonderful that I don't have to fear the future, Lord. I can choose faith over fear. I can choose resting in Jesus over running around worrying. I know that there will be hard times and bumps in the road along the journey, but I also know that as a Christian, I have nothing to fear. I can face the future with a smile on my face. You will never leave me or forsake me. Thank You, Lord. Amen.

You saw my body as it was formed. All the days planned for me
were written in your book before I was one day old.
PSALM 139:16 NCV

Creator God, You are really amazing. Before my mother even knew that I was growing in her belly, You knew. You decided the exact day that I would be born and You have already planned out all of my days. Why would I worry about next week or next year? Why should I fear? I have the God of the universe watching over my steps. You are in control. Thank You for this comforting truth. In Jesus' name I pray, amen.

In everything we have won more than a victory because of Christ
who loves us. I am sure that nothing can separate us from God's
love—not life or death, not angels or spirits, not the present
or the future, and not powers above or powers below.
Nothing in all creation can separate us from God's love
for us in Christ Jesus our Lord!
ROMANS 8:37–39 CEV

Father, I feel afraid sometimes when I think about the future.
I don't have any idea what will happen. I feel out of control. I
find comfort in knowing that no matter what good or bad the
future holds, You will never leave me. Your love is forever. You
promise Your children that nothing can separate us from Your
love. Nothing. Not even the future with all of its unknowns. You
will still be loving me in five years, ten years, and for all eternity.
Wow! Amen.

MY GIFTS—
THE POWER OF SERVICE

The Bible teaches us that each and every Christ follower has been given unique spiritual gifts. If we all had the same exact strengths and weaknesses, wouldn't the Church be kind of boring? Instead, God decided to make the body of Christ interesting! Some have the gift of teaching. They teach God's truths. Others have mercy. They meet needs. Still others have the gift of helps. They help out and make things happen, but they don't have to be at center stage. Some people can tell when something is just a little "off" with a message. This is the gift of discernment. One gift that is especially helpful to others is the gift of encouragement. Don't you love to be around an encourager? Do you know your own spiritual gifts? You can read about gifts in Romans and 1 Corinthians in your Bible. You will never feel more satisfied than when you are using your gifts for the Lord!

We all have different gifts, each of which came because of the grace God gave us. The person who has the gift of prophecy should use that gift in agreement with the faith. Anyone who has the gift of serving should serve. Anyone who has the gift of teaching should teach. Whoever has the gift of encouraging others should encourage. Whoever has the gift of giving to others should give freely. Anyone who has the gift of being a leader should try hard when he leads. Whoever has the gift of showing mercy to others should do so with joy.

ROMANS 12:6–8 NCV

Dear heavenly Father, it's amazing the way You put gifts in Your people. You didn't make us all just alike. You created us like a body with many different parts that all work together. Help me to discover my spiritual gifts, Father, and then use them for Your glory. I'm not always sure what I would be good at, but You can guide me and direct me to the perfect ways to serve. Give me opportunities to participate in serving You. I love You, Lord. Amen.

> Each of you should use whatever gift you have received to serve
> others, as faithful stewards of God's grace in its various forms.
> 1 PETER 4:10 NIV

Dear God, I've learned about tithing and making sure that I'm
using my money wisely. I suppose I should do the same thing
with all of the gifts You have given me—even my spiritual gifts. If
I have received a gift from You that I don't put into practice and
use in service to You, am I wasting it? I guess I am. Help me to
faithfully give of my time and my talents in the same way that I
have learned to give of my money. Amen.

> Just as our bodies have many parts and each part has a special
> function, so it is with Christ's body. We are many parts
> of one body, and we all belong to each other.
> ROMANS 12: 4–5 NLT

God, sometimes I look down on other Christians just because their
gifts are different from my own. This is wrong and I don't want to
do this anymore. Some people have the gift of helps, and they are
meant to work behind the scenes. Not everyone is a teacher. Some
have the gift of mercy. This doesn't make them weak. It means
You have given them an extra ability to see others in need. Wow,
God. It's pretty cool how You've made us all different. Help me to
value others' gifts and to use my own in order to serve the body of
Christ. Amen.

Open your homes to each other, without complaining.
1 PETER 4:9 NCV

God, whatever I have is Yours. Help me to see all of my belongings and gifts as Yours and to never complain about sharing them with others. Were it not for Your mercy and grace, I would have nothing. I would be nothing. May I use all of my resources for Your glory. May I see everything I have as a tool to be used for You. Whether it means hosting a Bible study in my home or helping someone who is struggling in a school subject that comes easy to me, may I honor You by using my gifts and resources. Amen.

God is not unjust; he will not forget your work and the love
you have shown him as you have helped his people
and continue to help them.
HEBREWS 6:10 NIV

Lord, You see everything that we do. You are all-knowing and ever present. You are just. You see my good deeds that are done in Your name. You will not forget my service for the kingdom. One day You promise to reward me in heaven. I will lay all my crowns before the Savior. I will return all my rewards to Him. May I do good while I'm on this earth. May I serve others with kindness and compassion. May I give extravagantly. In Jesus' name I pray, amen.

"And whoever wants to be first must be your slave—
just as the Son of Man did not come to be served,
but to serve, and to give his life as a ransom for many."
MATTHEW 20:27–28 NIV

Lord Jesus, You could have come as a majestic king, but instead You came to serve people. You are the Son of God, and yet You were not out to draw attention to Yourself. You healed the sick and taught on the hillside. You ate with people others wouldn't dare to even be seen with, and You gave Your very life. You paid the ultimate price, gave the ultimate gift. You died for us. Oh, Lord, may I be Your servant. May I be found faithful in serving You. Amen.

But you know that Timothy has proved himself,
because as a son with his father he has served
with me in the work of the gospel.
PHILIPPIANS 2:22 NIV

Dear God, I'm encouraged when I read about Timothy in the Bible. He was young and yet You chose to use him in big ways. He helped to spread the good news of the Gospel. He had grown up learning about You from his mother and grandmother. He was prepared and You used him. Prepare me for the work You have for me, God. Help me to learn and to be ready when You call. Amen.

Then a despised Samaritan came along, and when he saw the man, he felt compassion for him. Going over to him, the Samaritan soothed his wounds with olive oil and wine and bandaged them. Then he put the man on his own donkey and took him to an inn, where he took care of him.

Luke 10:33–34 NLT

Dear Lord, some have been given the gift of mercy. The Good Samaritan showed great mercy for a man lying on the side of the road. Others had passed him by, but not the Samaritan. He took the man to an inn and cared for him. Even when he had to leave, he paid someone to continue looking after this wounded person. Make me more like the Good Samaritan. May I show mercy when I see anyone in need. In Jesus' name I pray, amen.

"Whoever serves me must follow me; and where I am, my servant also will be. My Father will honor the one who serves me."
JOHN 12:26 NIV

Jesus, I will follow You. I will follow even if no one goes with me. I will follow You on good days and bad days. I want to serve You all the days of my life. Lead me. I don't always know where to go or who to talk to, and so I will just walk in Your footprints. I will follow You and seek to be used of You wherever You lead. Amen.

"In the same way, let your good deeds shine out for all to see, so that everyone will praise your heavenly Father."
MATTHEW 5:16 NLT

Dear God, help me to do good things not so that people will notice me but so that they will see You in me. I want to shine for You. I want to bring glory to Your name because You are a good God and You desire that everyone will come to know You. Help my actions to point the way to a loving God so that others will come to know You as their Lord and Savior. Amen.

God gave these four young men wisdom and the ability to learn many things that people had written and studied. Daniel could also understand visions and dreams.

DANIEL 1:17 NCV

Lord, You used Daniel and his three friends. They were young like me. You gave them wisdom and gifts. You used them in a mighty way. Because of their faith in You, eventually the king began to worship You and he changed the laws of his kingdom. He recognized that You were the one true God because You saved the boys from death in the fiery furnace. I want to be used in big ways even while I'm young. Use me, Lord. I am Your servant. Amen.

Do your work willingly, as though you were serving the Lord himself, and not just your earthly master. In fact, the Lord Christ is the one you are really serving, and you know that he will reward you.

COLOSSIANS 3:23–24 CEV

Dear Jesus, I get tired of going to school and doing all my class work and homework. I dread doing my chores at home, too. Please help me to have a better attitude. I want to work as if I'm doing all those jobs for You and not for my teachers or parents. In all things I will choose to serve the Lord. I want to honor You with my work and with my attitude toward it. Help me to do better with this. Amen.

Then Aaron's sister Miriam, a prophetess, took a tambourine in her hand. All the women followed her, playing tambourines and dancing.
EXODUS 15:20 NCV

God, I never really think of art as a gift. But some people are definitely better at it than others. I believe You must have given some people special talents in this area. Singing and dancing can be used for Your glory. So can painting or sculpting. Any kind of creativity comes from You and should be used for You. Help me to use my artistic gifts for You, Lord, and help me to appreciate the gifts of others around me, whatever they might be. Amen.

But Moses said to the LORD, "Please, Lord, I have never been a skilled speaker. Even now, after talking to you, I cannot speak well. I speak slowly and can't find the best words."
EXODUS 4:10 NCV

God, You called Moses to speak to the people. You used him as a leader even though he had a speaking problem. I don't feel like I'm very good at much of anything. Sometimes people even laugh at me. I wonder if anyone ever laughed at Moses when he was speaking slowly or searching for the right words. It helps me to know that You can use us if we are willing, even if we're not the most gifted of all people. Amen.

The word of the LORD came to me, saying, "Before I formed you in the womb I knew you, before you were born I set you apart; I appointed you as a prophet to the nations."

JEREMIAH 1:4–5 NIV

Lord, You set apart the prophet Jeremiah. You did it while he was in his mother's womb. You create and You gift Your children. Like an artist, You make each of Your masterpieces a bit different from the next. I imagine You there in the heavens thinking of me before I even existed in my parents' minds. Scratching Your head and smiling, You chose some special gifts for me. Reveal them to me, Lord. Use me, I pray. I love knowing that You made me just as I am for a special purpose in Your world. Amen.

Suddenly, a man with leprosy approached him and knelt before him. "Lord," the man said, "if you are willing, you can heal me and make me clean."

MATTHEW 8:2 NLT

Jesus, You healed the man with leprosy. You healed him because he had great faith in You. He believed. You are looking for people with faith, people who have no doubt that You are the Savior of the world. I want to be such a person. I sometimes doubt. I ask that You take away my doubt and replace it with faith like the leper had, faith that believes You can do the impossible. Give to me the gift of faith, I ask. Amen.

MY HABITS—
THE POWER OF GOOD CHOICES

Choices are the little life decisions you get to control, like choosing to have chicken strips instead of a hamburger, or a fruit cup instead of fries. Some good choices have a happy ending, like a trip to the park or mall for being dependable with schoolwork, while bad choices, like showing disrespect to your mom or dad, may mean temporarily losing something you like.

Imagine having two banks and a lot of pennies. One bank is only to be used when making good choices. The other bank is for bad choices. If you put "habit pennies" in your banks for a month, how many do you think you'd have in each bank?

We become more like the choices we make. The more good choices you make, the more good habits you'll have. The more bad choices you make, the more bad habits will come between you and your family, teachers, and God.

The older you get, the more choices you'll get to make. If you learn the power of good choices now, you can build good habits that hold on to relationships in the future. What's your choice?

Imitate God, therefore, in everything you do,
because you are his dear children.
EPHESIANS 5:1 NLT

Dear God, You always make the best choices. You made a way for me to be Your friend. I don't always make good choices. I also have some bad habits. Help me pay attention to the things You do so I can do them, too. If I can be more like You, then I can learn good habits. I want my choices to make You happy. I want my habits to be noticed for how they seem like something You would do. Amen.

[Jesus said,] "I tell you the truth,
everyone who sins is a slave of sin."
JOHN 8:34 NLT

Dear God, sometimes I just don't get it. I make a bad choice and right away I'm upset with myself. Some people call the feeling you get when you sin your conscience, and others call it the prompting of the Holy Spirit. All I know is I usually wish I hadn't done whatever it was I did. Sometimes I feel like I can't even stop myself from making a bad choice. Help me start making good choices, because I don't want the bad choices to make me someone I'm ashamed of. Amen.

The temptations in your life are no different from what others experience. And God is faithful. He will not allow the temptation to be more than you can stand. When you are tempted, he will show you a way out so that you can endure.

1 CORINTHIANS 10:13 NLT

Dear God, temptation comes when I think a bad choice is a good decision. Many bad choices seem like a lot of fun. Some seem harmless. Sometimes friends want me to do what they do. When I know the right thing to do—help me to do it. Remind me to talk to You about any temptation I face, because it seems like it's always easier to do the wrong thing, and I don't want to. I will always need Your help. Amen.

A wise son heeds his father's instruction,
but a mocker does not respond to rebukes.
PROVERBS 13:1 NIV

Dear God, there are times when I'm not sure my parents really understand what it's like to be me. They tell me to do things, or not do things, and I can't seem to figure out why it's so important. I know they're supposed to help me learn, so help me pay attention and be patient while I wait to really understand why what they say is so valuable. You want me to listen to my parents, and I need You to help me really listen and then obey. Amen.

For the wages of sin is death, but the free gift of God
is eternal life through Christ Jesus our Lord.
ROMANS 6:23 NLT

Dear God, You sent Jesus to pay the price for my bad choices. You call them sins. You also said if I were paid for making bad choices, the payment would be death. That's a payment I don't want. I know You want me to make good choices, and I'm thankful You offer eternal life when I make one really good choice—accepting the gift of Jesus. After that choice, help me continue to make good choices. I know that's what You want, so help me want it, too. Amen.

Let's not get tired of doing what is good.
At just the right time we will reap a harvest
of blessing if we don't give up.
GALATIANS 6:9 NLT

Dear God, sometimes I make good choices because
I want other people to notice. It's nice when they tell
me I'm doing a good job. But that can't be the only
reason to make good choices. Maybe I'm supposed
to make good choices because You asked—even
when no one notices, and even when I don't think
there's any benefit. Doing the right thing is hard
work, and sometimes there's no one to remind me
to pay attention to the choices I make. Wait, You're
always there. Help me remember. Amen.

> Trust in the LORD with all your heart;
> do not depend on your own understanding.
> PROVERBS 3:5 NLT

Dear God, You said lying is a bad choice. Because You said it, I know it's true, but I see people lie all the time and it doesn't seem like anything bad happens to them. I see kids cheat in school and get away with it. I've even seen people get hurt and no one seems to care. Are there really kids who follow You? Maybe I don't have to understand everything to know You want me to be truthful, honest, and kind. Because You know more than me, help me trust You to be right in everything. Amen.

> Seek his will in all you do, and he will show you which path to take.
> PROVERBS 3:6 NLT

Dear God, You want me to follow You without ever hearing Your voice. Talking to people is a lot easier than trying to guess what they're thinking. Since I can't talk to You face-to-face, help me to want to pray and then to read the Bible. You wrote some pretty amazing things for me to learn. Maybe someday I can talk to You like I do with my friends, but until then, help me to learn what You've said so I can do what You ask. Amen.

You must remain faithful to the things you have been taught.
You know they are true, for you know you can
trust those who taught you.
2 TIMOTHY 3:14 NLT

Dear God, there are people in my church who help me learn more about You. I have to be honest; there are times when I don't pay as much attention as I should, but there are other times when what I learn is something new that can help me make good choices and develop better habits. You want me to do certain things, and I want to do what You want. I know I can't do it without You. Amen.

Just as you accepted Christ Jesus as your Lord,
you must continue to follow him.
COLOSSIANS 2:6 NLT

Dear God, You want people to come to You just as they are, but I'm also learning that You don't want them to stay like they were. If You didn't want them to change, then why would they need to be saved? I don't want to just say I love You and then act like You don't matter. That just doesn't make sense. I want to make the same choices You would make. Help me do that. Amen.

Whatever you do or say, do it as a representative
of the Lord Jesus, giving thanks through him
to God the Father.
COLOSSIANS 3:17 NLT

Dear God, when people hear me say I'm a Christian,
I wonder what they think. Do they expect me to be
different? Would they be surprised to notice more
good choices than bad? I want to be like You. I want
others to see that You make a difference in people
who follow You. When I make bad choices, it makes
You sad, and it makes other people think I'm not
following You very well. Help me to remember that
the main job of a follower is to follow. Amen.

*Remain in fellowship with Christ so that when he returns,
you will be full of courage and not shrink
back from him in shame.*
1 JOHN 2:28 NLT

Dear God, what would it be like if You came for a visit? You might ask me hard questions about the choices I'm making, the things I do when I'm with my friends, and the things I think about when I'm all by myself. What would I say? I don't want to make bad choices thinking You might not be looking. You aren't just my friend; You're the One who saved me. Help me honor You in every choice I make. Amen.

* * *

I can do everything through Christ, who gives me strength.
PHILIPPIANS 4:13 NLT

Dear God, I keep hearing that some people don't think someone my age can make good choices. Some people just seem to want to try to help kids after they've made bad choices. I know I'm not an adult yet, but I think making good choices would be better than going through the trouble that always seems to come with bad decisions. You promised to help me, and I believe You can make me strong enough to say no to what I shouldn't do and yes to the things You want me to do. Thanks for Your help. Amen.

Wise choices will watch over you.
PROVERBS 2:11 NLT

Dear God, I'm not sure why I didn't think of this before, but the people I trust most are people who make good choices. It can be fun hanging out with people who make bad choices, but I usually get in trouble, and I'm never sure they can be trusted. It seems like good choices make it possible for my mom and dad to trust me. When I do the right thing, we don't argue as much. When I do the right thing, I believe You're happy. Help me trust You to help me make good choices. Amen.

MY HEART—
THE POWER OF A GENTLE SPIRIT

The Proverbs 31 woman is famous among those who read the Bible. She's the type of woman we should all seek to be. She's a hard worker. She treats her husband with respect and takes good care of her children. She is respected. She has a kind and gentle spirit. Even though you are young, you are learning how to be a godly young lady and one day a godly woman. It's important to take note of what God desires to see in the life of a Christian woman. These same traits are ones you can begin developing in your life even now. Responsibility means getting your schoolwork turned in on time and doing your chores at home without having to be reminded. And it's never too early to work at having a gentle spirit. Gentleness doesn't always come naturally, but God can create a gentle, loving spirit in you if you ask Him to and if you seek to follow His ways.

Love is patient and kind. Love is not jealous,
it does not brag, and it is not proud. Love is not rude,
is not selfish, and does not get upset with others.
Love does not count up wrongs
that have been done.
1 CORINTHIANS 13:4–5 NCV

Dear Jesus, fill me with love. You are the source
of all love. The Bible says that God is love. I have
experienced that unconditional, saving love of
Yours. Now let me show it to others. Give me
patience. Make me kind. Fill me with joy for others
instead of jealousy. Keep me from being prideful
or bragging. Make me tolerant rather than quick
to grow angry. Most of all, I ask that I be quick to
forgive, not keeping track of others' wrongs. I want
to show love. Fill me with Your love that it might
overflow from my life. Amen.

A gentle answer will calm a person's anger,
but an unkind answer will cause more anger.
PROVERBS 15:1 NCV

Dear God, I know that a godly woman controls her anger.
Sometimes people make me really mad! I pray that You will always
give me a gentle answer. I pray that You will set a guard over my
tongue so that I think before I speak. I know that if I get angry
with someone who is already stirred up, it will just cause the
person to get even madder. Nothing good comes from an angry
response. Help me, Lord. This is a challenge for me. Amen.

Do everything without complaining or arguing.
PHILIPPIANS 2:14 NCV

Dear Lord, no one likes a complainer. When I'm around one for
very long, I begin looking for an escape route! Please never let me
fall into the bad habit of whining and arguing. Certainly everyone
argues sometimes, but I don't want it to be a regular thing in my
life. Give me patience with others. And help me to focus on all my
blessings instead of what's going wrong in my day. Amen.

And she helps the poor and the needy.
PROVERBS 31:20 CEV

Dear God, give me a heart for those in need. There are so many people who have far less than I do. Provide opportunities for me to serve those who are less fortunate than me, whether it's through my church or in my community. May I serve them in Jesus' name. When basic needs are met, then people wonder why anyone would care enough to meet their needs. It's then that the Gospel can be shared and understood. Help me to give feet and hands to Your good news. Help me to put my faith into action rather than just talking about it. Amen.

Love is more important than anything else.
It is what ties everything completely together.
COLOSSIANS 3:14 CEV

Dear God, it seems that love is a lot like glue. It binds everything together. It's the most important thing. You tell me in Your Word that there are peace, love, and joy, and that the greatest of these is love. May I show love to everyone I meet. Sometimes it's hardest to show love to those who are closest in our lives—our family and close friends. Make a change in my heart today, Father. May I honor You by loving others well. In Jesus' name, amen.

> The people I treasure most are the humble—
> they depend only on me and tremble when I speak.
> ISAIAH 66:2 CEV

Lord, I put my trust only in You. I've tried trusting others, but sometimes they let me down. That's just because they are human. You never fail. You never leave or forsake me. I have the utmost respect for You, Father. You are perfect in every way and I fear You. I have a healthy fear of You, Lord. I also know that You are my Abba Father, my Daddy. Create in me a humility that is obviously from You. May others see You in me. Amen.

> I am not trying to please people. I want to please God.
> Do you think I am trying to please people? If I were doing that,
> I would not be a servant of Christ.
> GALATIANS 1:10 CEV

Dear Lord, I want to be a girl who is pleasing to You. I want to honor You in all that I do and say. In this world, we have to make a choice as to who we are trying to please. It's easy to get caught up in trying to please my friends, teammates, or classmates. But I am a servant of Jesus Christ. Regardless of what the world asks of me, I will follow You alone. May You be pleased with me, God. Amen.

"I have told you all this so that you may have peace in me. Here on earth you will have many trials and sorrows. But take heart, because I have overcome the world."
JOHN 16:33 NLT

Dear Jesus, You are my peace. Even though life is filled with sad times and trials, I know that I can always find peace when I lay my head on my pillow at night. I can always find it in You. The world is a tough place. It has been that way since sin came in through Adam and Eve's disobedience in the Garden of Eden. One day everything will be perfect again in heaven. For now, bless me with peace even in the midst of trials. Thank You, Father. Amen.

> When she speaks, her words are wise,
> and she gives instructions with kindness.
> PROVERBS 31:26 NLT

Dear God, I want to grow up to be a Proverbs 31 woman. What a model woman she is for all young girls. Please help me to gain wisdom through Your Word and through listening to and learning from older girls and women who are Christians. I want to be wiser than my years. Give me a kind spirit also, Father. Wisdom and kindness will serve me well in life. In Jesus' name I pray, amen.

> They must not slander anyone and must avoid quarreling. Instead,
> they should be gentle and show true humility to everyone.
> TITUS 3:2 NLT

Dear God, I struggle with pride. Maybe everyone does. It's a human problem. My old sinful nature tries to come out at times. I want the attention and the praise of others. Replace my pride with humility. Replace my harshness with gentleness. Create in me a clean and pure heart that avoids gossip and arguing. These things are not of You. In Jesus' name I ask You to change me. Amen.

In the same way, the women are to be worthy of respect, not malicious talkers but temperate and trustworthy in everything.
1 TIMOTHY 3:11 NIV

Lord, we girls have a tendency to be chatty. Help me to stay far away from gossip or from any talk that is dirty or inappropriate. I know I'm building a reputation for myself. I don't want to be seen as someone who stirs up trouble or starts rumors. I want to be stable and honest and trustworthy. There is great power in my words. Help them to be wholesome and good. Amen.

Do not make friends with a hot-tempered person, do not associate with one easily angered, or you may learn their ways and get yourself ensnared.
PROVERBS 22:24–25 NIV

Dear Jesus, help me to choose the right friends. If I associate with hot-tempered girls and boys, I may pick up their habits. I don't want to be someone who gets mad easily. That is no way to live. Set a guard over my heart and my lips, Father. Help me to keep my temper under control. Help me to conform to Your perfect will, which is always good and pleasing to You. Amen.

> Then the LORD God said, "It is not good for the man to be alone.
> I will make a helper who is right for him."
> GENESIS 2:18 NCV

God, You created man and then You made the decision to create woman also. Females are different from males. I like being a girl! We are more emotional and sensitive usually. We like different things than boys. I want to grow up to be a godly woman in Your sight. Help me to be a godly girl and to learn Your ways and how to please You, Father. In Jesus' name I pray, amen.

> A kind woman gets respect, but cruel men get only wealth.
> PROVERBS 11:16 NCV

Dear Lord, give me a kind heart. It's easy to be kind to my friends and to those who treat me nicely. It's harder to be kind to those who act ugly or don't treat others the way they should. I know that no matter how someone treats me, You tell me to turn the other cheek and to be kind in return. Help me to be kind so that I will be respected among my classmates and friends. I want to stand out as a Christian. Amen.

"The LORD your God is with you; the mighty One will save you.
He will rejoice over you. You will rest in his love;
he will sing and be joyful about you."
ZEPHANIAH 3:17 NCV

Dear Lord, rejoice over me. Sing over me. Let me find my rest
in You. It can be tiring being a girl. There's a lot of drama at
school. There are mean girls who say mean things. There are
bullies, Father. I seek to rest in Your presence. It's good to be Your
daughter and to always be able to seek refuge from the world
simply by calling on my Father's name. You delight in me. What a
privilege to be a daughter of the one true God! Amen.

MY IDENTITY—
THE POWER OF WHO I AM IN CHRIST

Have you ever thought about what you are? Sure, you have a name, and that helps everyone relate to you, but you're more than a name. You're someone's child, grandchild, cousin, student, friend, neighbor, study partner, guest, or babysitter.

As a Christian, you're something more than that. Who you are is a child of God. He loves you and has a plan for you to bring honor to the family name.

It's easy to forget who God says you are and live like there's no real difference between who you are and those who don't follow Jesus. Did you know that God says there should be a big difference? Did you know that He wants you to be different?

It can be hard to follow God when we don't know who God says we are. He described us as people who make a difference, people wise enough to know there's more to life than the tough things we face today, people who are compassionate enough to understand that people need to know about the God who makes us—different.

*Since you have been raised to new life with Christ,
set your sights on the realities of heaven, where Christ sits
in the place of honor at God's right hand.*
COLOSSIANS 3:1 NLT

Dear God, You have the best future planned for me. I really don't know what heaven is going to be like, but if You planned it, it must be pretty special. After all, You made Alaska, the clownfish, and redwood trees. Every time I go to the zoo I think about how creative You are. Each animal is so different, and yet You thought of what each one would be like. The God who made a lemur can be trusted with knowing the best way to create heaven. Right now? I'm thinking about being where You are. Amen.

*I am certain that God, who began the good work within you,
will continue his work until it is finally finished
on the day when Christ Jesus returns.*
PHILIPPIANS 1:6 NLT

Dear God, some days I want to give up on me, but You never do. I'm in the middle of a makeover, and I can't wait to see what You come up with. When I get my hair cut, the stylist asks me to move my head one direction or another. She knows how to give me a haircut, but I need to cooperate. That's just like You. As You work to change me, help me to cooperate. You see my potential. You know the possibilities. You never give up on me. That's awesome. Amen.

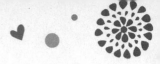

We are Christ's ambassadors; God is making his appeal through us.
We speak for Christ when we plead, "Come back to God!"
2 CORINTHIANS 5:20 NLT

Dear God, You gave me good news to share. When I get a good grade on my report card, I want people to know. When I finish reading a book that seems hard, I want to celebrate. The words You put in the Bible are good news. Help me read them and ask questions about what I don't understand, and then whenever I can, help me to be just as excited when I share the news that You offer forgiveness and love to everybody, even those I don't think would be interested. Help me be Your ambassador. Amen.

Such things were written in the Scriptures long ago to teach us.
And the Scriptures give us hope and encouragement as we wait
patiently for God's promises to be fulfilled.
ROMANS 15:4 NLT

Dear God, Your promises are on the way. Because You're God, You keep every promise You make. Sometimes it seems like it can take a long time for some promises to come true, but when You promised Noah You would never again send a flood that covered the whole earth, You kept Your promise. When You said the Messiah (Jesus) would come, You kept that promise, too. You said we should be encouraged because even more promises will be kept. I believe You will do what You said You would do. Amen.

Since God chose you to be the holy people he loves, you must clothe yourselves with tenderhearted mercy, kindness, humility, gentleness, and patience.

COLOSSIANS 3:12 NLT

Dear God, You're my Teacher. When someone gets in trouble, it's easy for me to think they deserve it, but when You offer forgiveness, I begin to think You look at things differently. When it would be easy to be rude, You want me to be kind. When I want to point out the things I'm good at, You want me to be humble. When I might want to answer roughly, You ask me to be gentle. When people seem slow, You want me to be patient. I've got a lot to learn. Thanks for being the best Teacher. Amen.

> Stop telling lies. Let us tell our neighbors the truth,
> for we are all parts of the same body.
> EPHESIANS 4:25 NLT

Dear God, You want me to tell the truth. You know, it's easy for humans to lie. We do it a lot. But You want me to be a truth-teller. Sometimes I get in trouble because when I tell the truth I'm also being honest about something I did wrong. Even then You want me to be honest. Maybe You do that so I don't have to live with secrets that make me unhappy. When I'm honest, I can strengthen my friendship with You and give others the chance to forgive me. Help me to always be truthful. Amen.

> [Jesus said,] "I have loved you even as the Father
> has loved me. Remain in my love."
> JOHN 15:9 NLT

Dear God, You really love me. The Bible tells me Jesus loves me just like God loved Jesus. That's a lot of love. It's easy to understand why God loves Jesus—He's perfect. But I'm not perfect. I make mistakes. Jesus came to show His love by paying for my sin by dying on a cross. Now that's love. Jesus rose from the dead and made it possible for me to live with Him in heaven someday. Now that's a gift. God said He would meet all my needs. Now that's amazing. Thanks, God. Amen.

God saved you by his grace when you believed.
And you can't take credit for this;
it is a gift from God.
EPHESIANS 2:8 NLT

Dear God, You give the gift of grace. Sin is
something that's easy to do but hard to stop. It
makes me feel bad, and I'm never sure how to make
up for it. When I believed in Jesus, You gave me
something I didn't deserve and could never earn.
Forgiveness and love. Because I can only accept
Your gifts, I feel thankful. You didn't have to offer
the gifts, but when I accept them I am closer to You,
and I want to stay close. Help me to always come
back to You, right where I should be. Amen.

We are citizens of heaven, where the Lord Jesus Christ lives.
And we are eagerly waiting for him to return as our Savior.
PHILIPPIANS 3:20 NLT

Dear God, You're waiting for me to come home. I live here now, but someday You want me to be with You in heaven. The Bible tells me it's where I really belong. Jesus lives in heaven and He promises to come back someday. That day will be awesome. I wouldn't even trade it for a day off school, a vacation, or a birthday party. I'm getting to know You more every day, but I can't wait to meet You in person. Help me get ready. Amen.

God knew his people in advance, and he chose them to become like his Son, so that his Son would be the firstborn among many brothers and sisters.
ROMANS 8:29 NLT

Dear God, You understand me. You made me, love me, and have things You want me to do. Before I was even born, You knew me. Before I could say my first word, You wanted me to be a part of Your family. When I believed in Jesus, You made that possible. I've met some of Your family, but if You have family all over the world, then I can't wait to meet everyone. No matter what anyone else thinks of me, I'm glad You understand me and choose to love me. Amen.

> Put on your new nature, created to be like God—
> truly righteous and holy.
> EPHESIANS 4:24 NLT

Dear God, You've given me an example to follow. I know I'm not there yet, but I want to be. I can't do it on my own and I need Your help. My new life is amazing, but when I make a mistake, I try to fix it on my own, run from it, or decide I just can't help it. Help me to keep coming back to You when I sin. You are willing to forgive me. Help me be willing to talk to You—especially about the hard stuff. Thanks for always listening. Amen.

• • • • • • • •

> [Jesus said], "I no longer call you slaves, because a master doesn't confide in his slaves. Now you are my friends, since I have told you everything the Father told me."
> JOHN 15:15 NLT

Dear God, You're my friend. You chose to be my best friend, so I want to do the same. I want our friendship to be close enough that I can tell You anything. Help me to read the Bible. All Your best advice is in there. It's awesome to know that the God who made everything wants to be my friend. Making friends can be hard, which makes it especially cool that You've always wanted to be my friend. I don't know why You keep amazing me, but You do. Amen.

To all who believed him and accepted him, he gave the right
to become children of God.
JOHN 1:12 NLT

Dear God, You made me Your child. I believed in Jesus and
accepted His forgiveness and life. That's when You called me
Your child. I know what it's like to be a child, but You're God. You
made this world. You told the stars where to stop in the night
sky. You made oceans, mountains, volcanoes, and the Grand
Canyon. You made animals, fish, and sunshine. You made me—
and then called me Your child. You took my old life and gave me
something new. You are so awesome. Thanks, Dad. Amen.

Anyone who belongs to Christ has become a new person.
The old life is gone; a new life has begun!
2 CORINTHIANS 5:17 NLT

Dear God, You made me new. When I accepted Jesus as my Savior,
You changed me. That must mean I'm supposed to be different. If
there isn't a difference in my life, maybe I'm not doing things right.
You want me to understand things from a new point of view. Being
kind, gentle, and loving is part of my new attitude. Help me practice
what I know to be true about the "new me." Help me stay away from
the things that remind me of what I used to be. Amen.

My old self has been crucified with Christ. It is no longer I who live, but Christ lives in me. So I live in this earthly body by trusting in the Son of God, who loved me and gave himself for me.
GALATIANS 2:20 NLT

Dear God, You want me to trust You. The Bible says You will help me make right choices, and I want to live for You. The Bible says my old life died, and I only want to remember what it's like to live the adventure You have for me now. It's easy to think about the way things used to be, so help me follow Your instructions. I believe You have something for me to do, so I will trust You to show me what that is, where I should go, and how I can serve You well. Amen.

MY QUIET TIMES—
THE POWER OF SOLITUDE

Quiet. It's often hard to find. This is a busy world with so much activity. Electronics are always beeping or ringing. Texting and social media take up a lot of time. It's amazing how the time goes by so quickly, and then it's time for bed. Sometimes it's hard to even remember what you spent all your time doing that day. Setting aside time to spend with God each day is really important for Christians. It's in these quiet times that God can speak to you and guide your thoughts. You've been given a great power source, but you must tap into it! Reading a passage of scripture each day—even a short one—and thinking on it will change your life. Talking to God and listening to His still, small voice are equally important. Never neglect your quiet times with God. They can make all the difference in the world.

Therefore confess your sins to each other and pray for each other so that you may be healed. The prayer of a righteous person is powerful and effective.

JAMES 5:16 NIV

Lord, as I sit quietly in Your presence, I lift up my family and friends to You. I call them by name and ask You specifically to meet their needs. As I speak the names of my loved ones, Father, I pray that You will hear my prayers and heal the hurts in these who are so dear to me. Help them. Comfort them. Love them with Your unfailing love, God. I lift up each need and place it before Your throne, knowing that You hear my requests. I thank You in advance for all that You will do. Amen.

Your word is a lamp that gives light wherever I walk.
PSALM 119:105 CEV

Where would I be without Your Word, Father? It gives me light that is needed to walk in a dark world day by day. It is a lamp to my feet. Wherever I go, whatever I do, Your Word provides a source of light that is not available to those who do not follow You. May I always be thankful for the Bible. May I spend time each day reading it so that I may never walk in darkness like those who don't know the one true God. Amen.

Is anyone among you in trouble? Let them pray.
Is anyone happy? Let them sing songs of praise.
JAMES 5:13 NIV

Lord, You tell me to come before You when I'm happy or when I'm sad. You want to hear from me no matter how I'm feeling. My quiet times with You are precious and priceless. You renew my spirit as I pray and read Your Word. Thank You that I can come to You every single day of my life, regardless of my circumstances or feelings. Amen.

"This, then, is how you should pray: 'Our Father in heaven,
hallowed be your name. . .' "
MATTHEW 6:9 NIV

You taught us how to pray, Jesus. You gave us the model to go by.
And the first thing You told us is to acknowledge the holiness of
Your Father. Holy is Your name. It is unbelievable that I'm allowed
to spend time with the most holy God. Let me never take that for
granted or push it to the end of my to-do list. Help me to set aside
quiet time each day. Amen.

Everything in the Scriptures is God's Word. All of it is useful
for teaching and helping people and for correcting them
and showing them how to live.
2 TIMOTHY 3:16 CEV

God, when I take time to read Your Word, I find great wisdom.
Your Word is full of truth that guides me in my decisions, my
friendships, my school day, and everything I do. Your Word
teaches and corrects me. On the pages of the Bible, I find Your
ways and Your desires for me. You have blessed me with the
freedom to read Your Word. May I honor Your Word by setting
aside time to read it daily. Amen.

> But they delight in the law of the LORD,
> meditating on it day and night.
> PSALM 1:2 NLT

Whether it's in the morning or at night or both, Lord, I love to read Your Word. There is so much power in the words on the pages of Your holy Bible. I am better and wiser and stronger after spending time reading Your Word. Create in me a deep desire to read the Bible. Help me to think about its words and to live by its principles. I love You, Lord, and I love Your Word. Amen.

● · ● · ● · ● · ●

> "And when you pray, do not keep on babbling like pagans,
> for they think they will be heard because of their many words."
> MATTHEW 6:7 NIV

God, even just a few moments with You is better than hours and hours with anyone else. You are my God. You created me and You know my heart and my needs. When I come before You, sometimes it's just a humble prayer to start my day, but I know that You hear me and You will answer. Thank You that I don't have to go on and on and on. You don't desire many words, just heartfelt ones. Amen.

Going a little farther, he fell with his face to the ground and prayed, "My Father, if it is possible, may this cup be taken from me. Yet not as I will, but as you will."
MATTHEW 26:39 NIV

God, it encourages me that even Jesus asked You to change His circumstances. He asked. You didn't answer by removing the cup. You had a plan, and His death was necessary in order to carry out that plan. Jesus had to go to the cross even though He asked You three times if there could be another way. Let this be a model for my prayer times. It's okay to ask You for something. It's okay to ask You to change a tough situation or something You are asking of me. But I must accept Your answer. I want only Your will. Amen.

After he had dismissed them,
he went up on a mountainside by himself to pray.
MATTHEW 14:23 NIV

Jesus, You went off by Yourself to pray to Your Father. You were around people much of the time, but You knew that solitude was extremely important as well. You were fully God and yet fully man. If You, the Son of God, took time for prayer, how much more should I? I find it hard to separate myself from my family and my friends. Give me a special place and time that I can set aside for my alone time with You. It is so valuable in my life. Amen.

In peace I will lie down and sleep, for you alone,
LORD, *make me dwell in safety.*
PSALM 4:8 NIV

God, You are my peace. You are the One who protects me while I sleep. Just before I go to bed each night, I love to spend a few moments with You. I just lift my prayer to You in those quiet moment, and I know that You hear me. I know that You watch over me as I sleep. Thank You, Father. In Jesus' name I pray, amen.

And the Holy Spirit helps us in our weakness. For example, we don't know what God wants us to pray for. But the Holy Spirit prays for us with groanings that cannot be expressed in words.
ROMANS 8:26 NLT

There are times, God, when I come before You and I don't have any words. I don't know what to say. Some days I'm just too burdened or sad. Other days the needs just seem so great that I can't put them into words. It's beyond me. It's too hard, too complicated. It's in those times that the Holy Spirit prays for me. The Spirit intercedes for me. The Spirit helps me. Knowing this truth is such a comfort to my soul. Amen.

By the seventh day God had finished the work he had been doing;
so on the seventh day he rested from all his work.
GENESIS 2:2 NIV

Lord, You rested after You created the world. You weren't tired. You never grow weary. I wonder if part of the reason You rested was to set an example for us humans. We need to rest. We need to take time to ourselves, time set aside to spend with You, time to pray and to seek You. You want us to work, but You also desire that we rest. Thank You for showing me this truth. May I live by it. Amen.

"But when you pray, go into your room, close the door and pray
to your Father, who is unseen. Then your Father, who sees
what is done in secret, will reward you."
MATTHEW 6:6 NIV

God, You want me to spend time with You. Just You and me. Father and child. It's in those times that I feel so close to You. Even when I don't feel it, I know it's true. You hear my prayers. You draw near to me when I draw near to You. You love to spend time with me and teach me truths from Your Word. Help me to be more faithful about my quiet times with You. My day always goes better when I start it out with You. Amen.

"And when you pray, do not be like the hypocrites, for they love to pray standing in the synagogues and on the street corners to be seen by others. Truly I tell you, they have received their reward in full."

MATTHEW 6:5 NIV

Heavenly Father, I don't have the right words. Sometimes I feel like I ramble when I come before You. I feel better when I remember that You are not concerned with my words. You see my heart. You just want me to come to You and be still and quiet before You. You remind me to listen rather than do all the talking when I pray. Thank You that I don't have to be perfect or use the perfect words. You love me just the way I am. You understand me, and You love to spend time with Your child. Amen.

MY SALVATION—
THE POWER TO RESCUE MY SOUL

When someone is employed, they get paid. That's the way we expect things to work, right? When adults work hard, they earn money for a job well done.

God does things differently. He has gifts to offer and He has the ability to rescue us from a sinful past, but He wants us to accept His offer first.

You have to understand you can never work hard enough to earn forgiveness. You can't buy eternal life. You just have to receive forgiveness and life as gifts from the God who loves you. Saying thanks is always a good response. Remember, if you have to work for a gift, then it's not really a gift.

When you ask God to rescue you, He also gives you everything you need to become more like Him. We know when we're really growing because our lives will show it. Galatians 5:22–23 (NLT) says, "[God's] Spirit produces this kind of fruit in our lives: love, joy, peace, patience, kindness, goodness, faithfulness, gentleness, and self-control." When you show these fruits in your life, then you are showing thankfulness for God's great gifts.

When God our Savior revealed his kindness and love,
he saved us, not because of the righteous things
we had done, but because of his mercy. He washed
away our sins, giving us a new birth and new
life through the Holy Spirit.
TITUS 3:4–5 NLT

Dear God, You are merciful. Your mercy shows up
when I go to my family and ask for forgiveness after
I've done something wrong and then feel bad about
it. You could punish me, but You forgive me instead.
Because I sin by making bad choices, You've offered
an entirely new life by showing mercy and loving
me enough to take an eraser to my list of sins. The
only things I know to add to what You give are
thankfulness and obedience. Let those be my gift to
You. Amen.

Whoever has the Son has life; whoever does not
have God's Son does not have life.
1 JOHN 5:12 NLT

Dear God, You offer life, and I accept that life. You said real life
is found in Jesus, and I invite Your Son to help me live more
like You. Even though some people live without loving Jesus,
You say that they aren't really living. I'm thankful You've offered
something more. It makes a difference in me. It makes a difference
in how I think of people I meet. It also makes a difference in how I
live. Continue to change me and make me new. Amen.

For God made Christ, who never sinned, to be the offering for our
sin, so that we could be made right with God through Christ.
2 CORINTHIANS 5:21 NLT

Dear God, You paid for something I was responsible to pay. Your
Word tells me that everyone sins. Your Word tells me that the only
payment I can expect from sin is death. Your Word also tells me
that Jesus never sinned so You accepted His sacrifice instead.
I'm sad Jesus had to die because I sin, but I'm thankful I can be
forgiven and accepted by You because of His gift. Jesus lives, and
He lives in me. Amen.

If we are living in the light, as God is in the light, then we have fellowship with each other, and the blood of Jesus, his Son, cleanses us from all sin.
1 JOHN 1:7 NLT

Dear God, You want me to spend time with those who follow You. I learn from others who have learned from You. Everyone learns best by reading Your Word. You bring us together because Jesus paid the price of forgiveness. Help me understand the value of people. You love each of us and offer the same gift to everyone. I don't know why someone would say no to Your gift. It would be awesome if everyone said yes to God. Amen.

The Lord isn't really being slow about his promise, as some people think. No, he is being patient for your sake. He does not want anyone to be destroyed, but wants everyone to repent.
2 PETER 3:9 NLT

Dear God, You are patient. Some people think there are too many bad things happening around the world. They wonder why You haven't come back. Some people have waited all their lives for You to return. It's just like You to be patient enough so that people who aren't following You can turn away from their sin and start to follow. I don't mind waiting to see You if it means more people can accept Your best gift. Thanks for being patient. Help me to be patient, too. Amen.

"There is salvation in no one else! God has given no other name under heaven by which we must be saved."
ACTS 4:12 NLT

Dear God, You are the ultimate God. No one else even comes close. You told us Jesus rescues us. You also said there was no one else in the entire world who could offer salvation. My sin can be forgiven only because Jesus died on the cross. I can spend forever with You only because Jesus didn't stay dead. Because I want to be with You in heaven, I shouldn't look anywhere else but Jesus to help me understand what I must do to follow You with everything I am. Today I choose to keep following You. Amen.

Just as you accepted Christ Jesus as your Lord,
you must continue to follow him.
COLOSSIANS 2:6 NLT

Dear God, You provide the best instructions. Your Word tell me that I shouldn't just accept Your gifts and then walk away. Your gifts change lives. Understanding how valuable Your gifts of love, forgiveness, and life really are makes me want to learn more about what You want me to do. If You can change my life, my heart, and my thoughts, then You can change anyone. It's like You've asked me to come along on a lifelong adventure, and You're the tour guide. Help me be willing to go where You lead. Amen.

Christ suffered for our sins once for all time. He never sinned, but he died for sinners to bring you safely home to God. He suffered physical death, but he was raised to life in the Spirit.
1 PETER 3:18 NLT

Dear God, Your Son, Jesus, paid for my sin by dying on a cross. His gift was so perfect it was the only sacrifice He would have to make to save me from all the sinful things I have ever done. His sacrifice was also enough to save anyone who asks. He came back to life after three days and returned to heaven. Jesus wants all of us to become Your friends. He wants all of us to spend forever with You in heaven. He wants to take me to see You. He's one amazing Son. I'm glad I know Him. Amen.

Salvation is not a reward for the good things
we have done, so none of us can boast about it.
EPHESIANS 2:9 NLT

Dear God, You did it all. You didn't need any help. You created this world with nothing but Your imagination. You made people so we could think, make decisions, and build things. Sometimes we think we're more important than You. We think we can make You do things for us, but Your Word tells us no one can brag because You came up with the idea of salvation. You said we couldn't earn it. You said salvation is not a reward for good behavior. We can come to You because You came for us. Now that's worth bragging about. Amen.

"For this is how God loved the world: He gave his one and only Son,
so that everyone who believes in him will not perish
but have eternal life."
JOHN 3:16 NLT

Dear God, You love me. It doesn't matter if I think I deserve it or not. Your Word says You loved me enough to send Your only Son to live on earth for a while. When I should have been punished for my sin, Jesus was punished instead. When I think of how Jesus died I wish things could have been different, but if Jesus hadn't paid the price then someday I would have to be punished for my sin, and I could never talk to You as a friend. Thanks for loving me that much. Amen.

*Jesus told him, "I am the way, the truth, and the life.
No one can come to the Father except through me."*
JOHN 14:6 NLT

Dear God, Your Son offers the only way to repair a soul. He is the only real truth. If I want real life, I discover it only by finding and following Him. In fact, I can only find You by finding Jesus. He is the only reason we can be friends. Jesus knows the way I need to go. He knows the truth that brings real freedom. He is where true life begins. Jesus made following easy. Help me stay focused on the journey ahead. Amen.

"The Son of Man came to seek and save those who are lost."
LUKE 19:10 NLT

Dear God, You found me. I didn't think I was hiding, but I also wasn't willing to be found. If I'm truthful, I think You knew where I was all along, but I kept looking at Your gifts and refused to accept them. Maybe I thought there would be a catch. Maybe I thought I wasn't good enough yet. Maybe I thought I would miss out on something if I spent too much time with You. I was lost. I wasn't good enough. I was found and You loved me anyway. I was never so happy to be found. Amen.

If you openly declare that Jesus is Lord and believe in your heart
that God raised him from the dead, you will be saved.
ROMANS 10:9 NLT

Dear God, Your Son is alive. Because He lives, I have been rescued.
It's easy to say I love Jesus when it's pretty clear He loved me
first. He died and rose again long before I was even born, but Your
Word tells me that even then You knew me. My brain is convinced,
my heart trusts, and my mouth should always be willing to talk
about Jesus, the One who saves. He has plans, He knows the way,
and He wants me to follow. Your Son has always been the best
leader. Amen.

"Everyone who calls on the name of the LORD will be saved."
ROMANS 10:13 NLT

Dear God, You make it easy to be saved. If I call on the name of the
Lord, I can be rescued, and I can claim all Your gifts as my own. I can
always ask for Your help. You don't keep salvation away from anyone.
No matter where I'm from, my family name, or the color of my skin,
You said I was part of the everyone who could call on You for rescue.
When I called, You answered. That was a good day. Amen.

"A person is made right with God by faith in Jesus Christ, not by obeying the law. And we have believed in Christ Jesus, so that we might be made right with God because of our faith in Christ."

GALATIANS 2:16 NLT

Dear God, You accepted me even when I didn't obey. I know You want me to obey, and Your Word says that my connection with You is repaired when I have faith in Your Son, Jesus. To have faith means to really believe, and I have to admit sometimes it's hard to believe in Someone I've never seen. But I see the way You care for me when the sun comes up each morning, when my family's needs are met, when I see people who smile. I want to be right with You, so I choose to believe. Amen.

MY SCHOOL—
THE POWER OF EDUCATION

Your school might be in a building with lots of other people, or it might be with a brother or sister in the living room. You might even attend a Christian or charter school. These are all places where you can learn, but they aren't the only places. School should be wherever you are.

Your mom or dad might give regular instruction. That's probably why God tells you to honor them. If you do it right, you will continue learning every day for the rest of your life. If that sounds boring, then you probably don't understand the real amazement in learning. Give it time; you might change your mind.

Some of the things we learn help us learn even more. Some things we learn will be interesting. Some things will be difficult to understand. Some things will be amusing. While education changes our minds, godly instruction changes our hearts, our lives, and our futures.

Let the wise listen to these proverbs and
become even wiser. Let those with
understanding receive guidance.
PROVERBS 1:5 NLT

Dear God, Your guidance is better than a map.
Your Word says that if I want to be wise, I have
to start with understanding. When You teach me,
help me understand what You're saying. I may have
questions, but You promise to guide me in the best
way. You begin by teaching me and then You show
me ways to use what I am learning. It seems like
wisdom is knowing the right thing to do and then
knowing how to do the right thing the right way.
That's what I want. Amen.

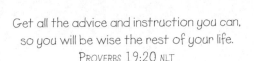

Dear God, You want me to use my mind. You want the truth I learn to change the way I think, act, and respond to You and others. You don't want me just to know facts. You want me to take what I know and use it for good. What I learn can help me honor my parents, obey Your commands, and help my friends. Because You want me to learn for the rest of my life, help me find ways to learn more about You today so that tomorrow I might be a little bit more like You. Amen.

Dear God, You want me to be a guardian of wise teaching. You have a lot to say in the Bible. The things You say are called the "key to life." When I read Your Word, it's like unlocking wisdom I can use to make good decisions. Teach me in Your "God school," and let me hold on to Your instructions for life. Help me know when I should share the things I learn. Help me be brave in sharing them. Help me never leave the truth found in Your Word. Amen.

> How much better to get wisdom than gold,
> and good judgment than silver!
> PROVERBS 16:16 NLT

Dear God, You know how costly gold is. Your Word tells me Your wisdom is worth even more. People who are wise not only know things but are really good at knowing how to handle difficult situations. It's not just that they are smart; they can help people to understand things without getting upset. People who have good judgment know when to stay away from something that might cause trouble. I want wisdom and good judgment. Help me find these treasures only You can provide. Amen.

> Wise people treasure knowledge,
> but the babbling of a fool invites disaster.
> PROVERBS 10:14 NLT

Dear God, You know the difference between knowledge and foolishness. Would You help me learn the difference? Your school is the best place to learn things that are true and honorable. Sometimes I say things I think are true, but I didn't really understand and then I look foolish. Sometimes what I say can hurt other people. I don't want to hurt others. Help me see my time with You as a treasure. Help me learn more about Your ways and use what I learn to speak wise words. Amen.

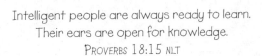

> Intelligent people are always ready to learn.
> Their ears are open for knowledge.
> PROVERBS 18:15 NLT

Dear God, You really want me to learn. When my teachers have something to share, help me to listen. When my Sunday school teacher shares from Your wise words, help me pay attention. When my mom or dad wants to teach me something, help me be an enthusiastic learner. Because I can learn anywhere, help me to look for chances to learn. It could be a new game, a math skill, or a way to serve You better. If intelligent people are always ready to learn, then help me be intelligent. Amen.

• · • · • · • · •

> Instruct the wise, and they will be even wiser.
> PROVERBS 9:9 NLT

Dear God, You know everything. I might know some things, but there's no one as wise as You. I want to be a lot wiser than I am right now. If I'm willing to learn, then maybe I can learn even more than I had planned. If I take initiative and read Your words often, the Bible says I will learn more. With You as my Teacher, I know I can learn and grow. What I learn will change me for the better. Your instruction will make me wise. I am Your student. Amen.

The LORD says, "I will guide you along the best
pathway for your life. I will advise you
and watch over you."
PSALM 32:8 NLT

Dear God, You protect me. Good teachers make sure
their students can learn in a protected environment.
You never said following You would be easy, but
You have offered to guide me, be my life adviser,
and keep an eye on me as I journey with You.
Nothing can happen to me without You knowing
it. Your Word tells me You always make sure I can
see clearly enough to take the next step. Guide me,
advise me, and watch over me as I take steps toward
You and away from the person I used to be. Amen.

Fear of the LORD is the foundation of wisdom.
Knowledge of the Holy One results in good judgment.
PROVERBS 9:10 NLT

Dear God, will You help me understand what Jesus would do?
I want good judgment. I want to be able to know when I should
leave a situation that doesn't honor You. I want to know the best
ways to help other people. I want to know how to show my parents
that I love and respect them. Help me know You more. Help me
love You deeply. Help me find wisdom by searching for You with
my heart, mind, soul, and strength. Amen.

How can a young person stay pure? By obeying your word.
PSALM 119:9 NLT

Dear God, You want me to be pure. Every day I want to learn more
about You. Every day I want to learn from You. Every day I want
to honor You by obeying the things I know You want from me. I
may not know everything, but as I've attended Your school, I have
gained an education that lets me know there are things I should
do and things I should avoid. Because I want You to continue
teaching me, I want to obey. Give me strength, because sometimes
it's really hard to do the right thing. Amen.

Show me the right path, O LORD;
point out the road for me to follow.
PSALM 25:4 NLT

Dear God, You already know the way that leads to my best future.
It's awesome to think that following You can lead to the life I was
made to live. This is why I need to learn from You. This is why
I need to obey. This is why I ask for directions. Every day I face
choices. Every choice leads me closer to or farther away from You. I
want the wisdom to recognize the way You lead. I want to be right in
the middle of the best things You have planned for me. Amen.

Lead me by your truth and teach me, for you are the God
who saves me. All day long I put my hope in you.
PSALM 25:5 NLT

Dear God, You can do it all. You rescue people from sinful lives.
You inspire hope in people who have none. You lead me and teach
me, but I need to recognize that Your words in the Bible are more
than inspirational thoughts—they are truth. You didn't just want
to give me life suggestions. When I am a student of Your truth, I
become more like You, love others in a way that honors You, and
learn in a way that make makes me a modern disciple. May my
choice to learn change me. Amen.

I will study your commandments and reflect on your ways.
PSALM 119:15 NLT

Dear God, You want me to be teachable. If it's on-the-job training, then I need to see how other trusted Christians handle tough problems. If it's learning directly from You, then I need to love Your Word. I can find out more about the qualities that make You so different from anyone else I know. I want to learn the things You ask me to do. Then when I study, I need to spend time thinking about how what I've learned can change who I am. Really knowing God changes something inside. Change me. Amen.

If you need wisdom, ask our generous God,
and he will give it to you. He will not rebuke you for asking.
JAMES 1:5 NLT

Dear God, You never get mad when I'm confused. I need wisdom, so I'm respectfully asking You for understanding. You love giving good gifts, and wisdom is one of the best. Sometimes it's easy to be confused because Your wisdom is so different than what I know. You want me to love those who hate me, forgive those who hurt me, and give when I don't have much. I'm sure You have good reasons, and that's why I need wisdom. Thanks for being willing to teach me. Help me understand and obey. Amen.

*Fear of the LORD is the foundation of true knowledge,
but fools despise wisdom and discipline.*
PROVERBS 1:7 NLT

Dear God, Your instructions require obedience. In school my
teacher will ask me to complete an assignment. It doesn't work
very well if I tell my teacher I just didn't feel like doing the
assignment. My teacher expects me to finish my work. If I don't,
then I get a bad grade. You expect me to obey Your instructions,
too. I need to start by first understanding that everything You do is
awesome. There is nothing You do that is less than awesome. Let
me learn and become wise. Help me be self-controlled enough to
complete Your assignments. Amen.

MY STRENGTH—
THE POWER OF JESUS CHRIST IN ME

Kids are constantly trying to get stronger! In PE class, they learn how to do exercises to strengthen their muscles. They get stronger in math and reading through studying. What about spiritual strength? Where does that come from? Making our bodies stronger is important, but the Bible tells us it's not as important as strengthening our hearts and minds. This kind of strength comes to us from God. When you pray to God for strength, He is glad to give it to you. When you read the Bible, you will gain courage by reading the stories of others who faced hard times and made it through them with God's help. One of the best preachers of all time, the apostle Paul, said it this way: "I can do everything through Christ, who gives me strength" (Philippians 4:13 NLT). Draw upon the strength of the Lord as you face the challenges ahead of you today.

Each time he said, "My grace is all you need. My power works best in weakness." So now I am glad to boast about my weaknesses, so that the power of Christ can work through me. That's why I take pleasure in my weaknesses, and in the insults, hardships, persecutions, and troubles that I suffer for Christ. For when I am weak, then I am strong.

2 CORINTHIANS 12:9–10 NLT

Dear God, I've been taught that it's good to brag, and I agree. But I love that I can brag about You! You give me strength when I am weak. You help me to overcome obstacles in my life, whether it's a tough class in school or a bully who insults me. You are a big, big God, and I will boast in Your power in my life! Amen.

For God has not given us a spirit of fear and timidity,
but of power, love, and self-discipline.
2 TIMOTHY 1:7 NLT

Wow! It's good to know that You have put in me a spirit of power, love, and self-discipline. When I'm nervous or shy, I can draw upon this source of power. I don't have to be bashful or scared. I have power from God in my heart. When I find it hard to love others around me or to forgive them, I can use the love that You have put in me. I will choose to have self-control because You discipline me, Father, in order that I may grow into the person I should be. Thank You for caring enough to give me these gifts. Amen.

The LORD is my light and my salvation—so why should I be afraid?
The LORD is my fortress, protecting me from danger,
so why should I tremble?
PSALM 27:1 NLT

Dear heavenly Father, I have no reason to fear. Sometimes I'm afraid of the dark of night. I find myself scared when I face certain girls in my classes or neighborhood. They intimidate me. Why should I fear them? They are just girls. You are the one true God. You cause the rain to fall and the sun to shine. I know my God is stronger than them! May I always find courage in You. Amen.

The men in the army were threatening to kill David with stones, which greatly upset David. Each man was sad and angry because his sons and daughters had been captured, but David found strength in the LORD his God.
1 SAMUEL 30:6 NCV

Dear Lord, even in the midst of trouble and trials, I can find strength in You. David went through some rough stuff, but the Bible calls him a man after God's own heart. Keep me close to Your heart, Father. Help me to have a hunger and thirst for Your Word. When I'm afraid, stand up for me and help me to feel Your strength so that I can be brave. Amen.

"Remember that I commanded you to be strong and brave. Don't be afraid, because the LORD your God will be with you everywhere you go."
JOSHUA 1:9 NCV

God, You have told Your people to be strong and to have courage. Just as You told this to Joshua many years ago, Your still, small voice tells me the same thing today. As I face people who treat me unfairly or a class that seems way too hard for me, I can call upon You to give me strength and make me brave. It's not a suggestion but a command. I will not be afraid because wherever I go, You are already there, making me stronger with Your presence. Amen.

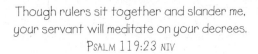

Though rulers sit together and slander me,
your servant will meditate on your decrees.
PSALM 119:23 NIV

Dear God, sometimes people say unkind things. They hurt my feelings. There are girls who stir up trouble by spreading rumors, gossiping, and even creating drama for no reason. Sometimes it hurts. That saying about sticks and stones hurting our bones but words not hurting. . .I don't think it's true. When other girls say mean things about me or laugh at me, it hurts deeply. Thank You for giving me strength to be kind even in the face of evil. I will choose to follow Your ways no matter what the cost. Amen.

I can do all this through him who gives me strength.
PHILIPPIANS 4:13 NIV

Dear heavenly Father, on my own I have no strength. Just as a computer that isn't plugged in can't work, I can't survive on my own. I must choose every day to tap into the power source of Your strength. Praying and reading Your Word make me feel like a different person. I sense that I am not all alone. I have You at my side. I can face anything that comes my way in the strength I have through Jesus. I am ready for good days and bad days as well. In His name I pray, amen.

The LORD is my light and my salvation—so why should I be afraid? The LORD is my fortress, protecting me from danger, so why should I tremble?
PSALM 27:1 NLT

God, I feel really safe when I'm in my bedroom or when I climb up in a tree house—there are places I just feel protected and as if nothing could get me even if it tried! The Bible says You are a fortress. You are a strong building that keeps Your children from danger. I may have to face some hard things in life, but I can always, always run and hide in my fortress to gain strength for the next battle. Thank You for being my strength. Amen.

Search for the LORD and for his strength; continually seek him.
1 CHRONICLES 16:11 NLT

Heavenly Father, there is no strength to be found in the world. It comes only through Jesus Christ. I have found that every time I try to do things on my own, I end up with a mess. I don't want to try to do life on my own anymore. On my own, I am very weak. I will face life in the strength of my Savior, who never lets me down and never turns away. I am strong because He is strong through me. Amen.

"The LORD is my strength and my defense; he has become my salvation.
He is my God, and I will praise him, my father's God,
and I will exalt him."
EXODUS 15:2 NIV

God, thank You for saving me through my faith in Jesus. It's great to know that when I go out to face my day, I have my Savior at my side. I am defended by the King of kings. He fights for me. He goes into battle for me. He is stronger than any force that may try to come against me. Thank You for the strength I have in Jesus. Amen.

"Don't be afraid, for I am with you. Don't be discouraged,
for I am your God. I will strengthen you and help you.
I will hold you up with my victorious right hand."
ISAIAH 41:10 NLT

Lord, give me strength to face this day. Calm my fears and replace
my discouragement with encouragement from Your Word. You
promise never to leave me. You say that nothing can separate
me from Your love. What courage I find when I remember that
promise! Be my strength today. I need You, God. Amen.

Be strong and take heart, all you who hope in the Lord.
PSALM 31:24 NIV

Dear Jesus, I'm scared of certain people and places, and sometimes
I fear the future. I'm thankful for Your friendship and that You are
my Savior. I find hope in You. Hope is important. Without it, life
would be unbearable. I choose this day to be strong and courageous
because I am a daughter of the Lord of lords. I am hopeful about the
future because You have great plans for me. Amen.

"You stretch out your right hand,
and the earth swallows your enemies."
EXODUS 15:12 NIV

God, You are very powerful. You have the strength to do anything that You desire to do. Please give me the strength I need to face my problems. They are not as big as world hunger. They may not seem like big problems, but they are big to me. I need Your strength to get through what I'm facing. It helps me to know that You hold the whole world in Your hands, and yet You see me and know my name. You are there to help me. In Jesus' name I pray, amen.

But God chose the foolish things of the world to shame the wise;
God chose the weak things of the world to shame the strong.
1 CORINTHIANS 1:27 NIV

Dear heavenly Father, You used Noah to build an ark. You used Moses to deliver the Ten Commandments. You chose a young shepherd boy named David to become king. You are not interested in how great people are, but how faithful and how willing they are to be used. You chose the weak to show the world how strong people can be when they have You in their hearts. Use me even in my weakness, I pray. You are my strength! Amen.

It is God who arms me with strength and keeps my way secure.
He makes my feet like the feet of a deer; he causes me to stand
on the heights. He trains my hands for battle;
my arms can bend a bow of bronze.
PSALM 18:32-34 NIV

I never think of myself as a warrior, God. But every day I go into
battle. There is a spiritual battle going on in the world between
darkness and light. Satan would love to trick Christians into
believing they are weak so that he can lead us off the right path.
Remind me today that You are my God and that You give me
strength for the battle. You are my strength in the fight. Amen.

MY TEMPER—
THE POWER OF SELF-CONTROL

Have you ever wondered why it's so easy to get mad, throw a fit, and say mean things? It's much harder to smile, help others, and be encouraging when you don't feel like it.

Everyone is born selfish. When we're little children we don't want to share toys. When a baby brother or sister comes home, we don't want to share Mom and Dad. When it's time to decide what to do, we want everybody to think our ideas are the best.

God wants us to be self-controlled. This means we are to be very careful how we respond to those around us. It means that anger shouldn't be our first choice. It means that we choose to share. It means that we look for good in the things others want to do.

Self-control is something God wants us to develop. Self-control is like developing spiritual muscles. It's how we show that God makes it possible to choose better ways to deal with how we feel.

Self-control always starts with the ability to make choices. We can choose to get angry or we can choose to forgive. Being self-controlled helps us become more like Jesus.

Make every effort to respond to God's promises. Supplement your faith with a generous provision of moral excellence, and moral excellence with knowledge, and knowledge with self-control, and self-control with patient endurance, and patient endurance with godliness, and godliness with brotherly affection, and brotherly affection with love for everyone.

2 PETER 1:5–7 NLT

Dear God, You said I can love others when I'm self-controlled. Your Word tells me that when I make right choices, choose a good response, am patient with others, choose Your way before mine, and care for others, I become someone who can really love people. Your Word tells me that the two greatest things I can do are to love God and then love everyone else. Help me be self-controlled so I can really love others the way You love them. Amen.

> A person without self-control is like a city
> with broken-down walls.
> PROVERBS 25:28 NLT

Dear God, You want me to cooperate with You. Self-control is one of the best ways I can do that. When I do what I want without learning what You have to say about my choice in Your Word, I get myself in trouble. I don't want to be someone who gets angry easily, thinking that things always have to go my way. Everything about my life works better when I choose to control my actions. You have rescued me and let me decide how close I come to being like You through my choices. Help me choose wisely. Amen.

> We are instructed to turn from godless living and sinful pleasures.
> We should live in this evil world with wisdom,
> righteousness, and devotion to God.
> TITUS 2:12 NLT

Dear God, following Your instructions makes me wise. Many people make bad choices. Their decisions hurt themselves and those they love. Your Word tells me to turn away from living that way. The best choices, the ones You tell me about in Your Word, show me that I should be wise and honorable, someone who follows You. Following You means I have choices to make. First, I choose not to do the things You've said are wrong. Second, I choose to do things that will please You. You've given me good instructions. Thanks. Amen.

> Don't you realize that in a race everyone runs,
> but only one person gets the prize? So run to win!
> 1 CORINTHIANS 9:24 NLT

Dear God, You want me to run Your race. I want the wisdom to know how to run well. I don't know anyone who starts a race wondering how they can make sure they come in last. The race You have for me is a race just for me. I don't compete with other people because then I might think I'm better—or worse—than others who run. You want every part of my racing ability to improve because I'm learning to follow Your coaching. Thanks for Your example. Watch me run. Amen.

> All athletes are disciplined in their training. They do it to win
> a prize that will fade away, but we do it for an eternal prize.
> 1 CORINTHIANS 9:25 NLT

Dear God, You have created a training program just for me. I choose to be self-controlled enough to accept training by reading Your Word with a good attitude. Help me choose daily training. Help me endure hard lessons. Help me put what I learn to the test. You've agreed to train me. I want to be disciplined enough to follow through each test, every struggle. Thank You for encouraging me to keep going. With Your help I can undergo the training and run Your race with courage, hope, and patience. Amen.

> Train yourself to be godly.
> 1 TIMOTHY 4:7 NLT

Dear God, You want me to respond like You. I can never be You, but I should find ways to help people see what You look like. If I'm rude, angry, and impatient, then people who know I'm a Christian will wonder if that's what You're like. If I'm kind, joyful, and patient, then people will think of You in a better way. It's the way You should be thought of. It's the way I want to be. I need the self-control required to show others how awesome You really are. Amen.

• • • • • • • • •

> Teach the older men to exercise self-control, to be worthy of respect, and to live wisely. They must have sound faith and be filled with love and patience.
> TITUS 2:2 NLT

Dear God, You've given me great examples of what self-control looks like. Some examples I see with my own eyes. Others I read about in Your Word. You say that people with self-control should be respected. I still need You to help me learn how to be self-controlled, but I'm thankful for those who love me and are patient when I blow it. With Your help I would like to grow up to become someone others can see as an example of what it looks like to follow You. Amen.

Don't love money; be satisfied with what you have.
For God has said, "I will never fail you.
I will never abandon you."
HEBREWS 13:5 NLT

Dear God, You want me to understand that You
are more important than money. Sometimes that's
hard to understand. I've seen things money can buy.
There are many things I want, and I need money
to buy them. But You are God. You created every
unique animal, vast oceans, breathtaking sunrises,
life-sustaining air, and delicate flowers. You never
charge for any of it. In fact, You give me eyes to see
and a brain to remember their beauty. Gifts of love,
joy, and peace are things money can't buy. Help me
to always be satisfied with Your gifts. Amen.

Stay away from every kind of evil.
1 THESSALONIANS 5:22 NLT

Dear God, You want me to respect Your protection. Sometimes it seems like there are too many things that You don't want me to do. It can be frustrating when I see other people do things You've told me to avoid. It could be that You are trying to protect me from bad influences, bad choices, and bad habits. You don't say no because You don't want me to enjoy myself, but because You always have something better if I am just willing to wait. Give me the courage to wait for Your best. Amen.

*Children, obey your parents because you belong
to the Lord, for this is the right thing to do.*
EPHESIANS 6:1 NLT

Dear God, You say parents are important. Self-control means making the choice to keep calm when it would be easy to lose my temper. I don't always agree with decisions my mom or dad makes. Your Word says that obeying my parents is the right thing to do. I honor my parents because I want to be more like You. If it's important to You, then let it be important to me. Help me be kind in my response and obedient in my actions, and let my face show Your joy. Amen.

You must all be quick to listen, slow to speak,
and slow to get angry.
JAMES 1:19 NLT

Dear God, You never want me to say something I'll regret.
Whenever I get angry I either say or think things that are unkind.
In Your Word You say I should listen more than I speak. There are
times when what I want to say right away is not the same thing I
would say if I waited. It's easy to get angry. It's easy to say the first
thing I think. If I don't have self-control, then I will never bring
honor to You. Please help me control my tongue. Amen.

Dear friends, never take revenge. Leave that to the righteous
anger of God. For the Scriptures say, "I will take revenge;
I will pay them back," says the LORD.
ROMANS 12:19 NLT

Dear God, You can take care of everything—even when I want to
help. It's easy to get angry. It's easy to want other people to suffer
for hurting me or someone I care about. It's hard to control my
actions even when I know You'll take care of things. When I want
to see someone punished, You want to show them love. You know
their story. All I know is they were rude. You have been kind to
me. It shouldn't surprise me when You are kind to others. Help me
trust Your decisions. Amen.

> Those who are peacemakers will plant seeds of peace
> and reap a harvest of righteousness.
> JAMES 3:18 NLT

Dear God, You want me to be a farmer. I may never grow wheat or corn, but You want me to plant seeds of peace and harvest a crop of godly goodness. Self-control helps me become someone who helps others see the value of peacefulness. I don't like it when things are out of control, so help me be a peace farmer. You can water the peace seeds and help them grow. I can't wait to see Your crop of godly goodness. It should be a great harvest. Thanks for giving me the help I need. Amen.

> Be careful how you live. Don't live like fools,
> but like those who are wise.
> EPHESIANS 5:15 NLT

Dear God, You don't want me to act foolish. That means You really care for me. You want me to be wise. That means You have a plan for me. I want to be careful in how I reply to my family, how I react to the things other people do, how I return good actions for bad intentions. I want Your name to be important to everyone. When I choose self-control, I will not act foolishly. I bring honor to Your name when I am careful in how I respond. Let me be careful—and wise. Amen.

God is not a God of disorder but of peace.
1 CORINTHIANS 14:33 NLT

Dear God, You want our world make sense. To do that You created day and night. You also created spring, summer, autumn, and winter. Everything You created works exactly like You wanted—except for people. You let us make choices. Sometimes we don't choose very well. We make a lot of really bad decisions. When we are self-controlled, we agree to cooperate with You in making peace from chaos. I want my decisions to make sense. I want to understand Your plans for me. I want to help other people see that a choice to follow You brings peace. Amen.

MY TIME—
THE POWER OF PRIORITIES

You only get twenty-four hours to spend each day. You don't get more hours, minutes, or seconds, and you don't get less. You can only make decisions about the time you actually have.

Most people will spend seven to nine hours sleeping. Then there is the time you take to eat, take a shower, decide what to wear, attend school, do homework, and talk with parents and friends. In the time that's left, you can make decisions about how those hours and minutes are used.

Saying you'd spend that time with God is a great decision, but how exactly will you do it? God's Word tells us there are many things He wants us to spend time developing. God doesn't leave us to guess.

You could spend time on your phone, the computer, and a video game, or you could discover the things that God says are really important. By discovering God's priority list, you can begin to spend time wisely.

Don't copy the behavior and customs of this world,
but let God transform you into a new person
by changing the way you think. Then you will
learn to know God's will for you, which is
good and pleasing and perfect.
ROMANS 12:2 NLT

Dear God, You say change is a good thing. You
want me to be more mature tomorrow than I am
today. Once upon a time I acted like a two-year-old.
I've grown up since then. If I acted like I was still
two years old, people would think something was
wrong with me. I can learn to understand what You
want me to do, but I need to grow up as a Christian.
Please change the way I think, give me wisdom, and
keep me away from the dumb stuff that keeps me
from growing up. Amen.

> "Seek the Kingdom of God above all else, and live righteously,
> and he will give you everything you need."
> MATTHEW 6:33 NLT

Dear God, You have given me one priority that is above all others. Seeking You is more important than anything else I can do. That means I need to make sure You are the most important part of my life. To spend time with You might mean I spend less time with hobbies, friends, and activities. It might mean I choose a time every day that I can spend reading Your Word and praying. It means doing things differently so I can live life differently. You've given me everything I need to seek You. Thanks. Amen.

> "Wherever your treasure is,
> there the desires of your heart will also be."
> LUKE 12:34 NLT

Dear God, You've given me truth about why priorities are important. Those things I believe are the most valuable are where I will always spend my time. If I make sports the most important thing, then that's where I will want to spend my time. That's true with friendships, family, and fun. No one wants to spend too much time doing something they don't think is worthwhile. I want my greatest treasure to be my highest priority. I want to know You so well that spending time with You is what I really want to do most. Amen.

"You must not have any other god but me."
EXODUS 20:3 NLT

Dear God, You want me to follow You on purpose. You don't want me to view anything else as more important. My priority needs to be You. I can choose a television show, clothes, sleep, my hair, hobbies, sports, collections, music, friends, texting, or even food as a priority. These can be good things that become more important than You. Anything that's more important than You is like a god. Your Word tells us not to follow other gods. Help me honor You above anything else I might enjoy. Amen.

Teach us to realize the brevity of life,
so that we may grow in wisdom.
PSALM 90:12 NLT

Dear God, You've given me time to become wise. Help me learn from You. Wisdom is a priority because without it I have no idea how to follow You. I could sing songs about You and feel good about the fact that You exist, but without wisdom I'm not sure what else I'm supposed to do. Eternity is forever, but each day is an opportunity to learn more about the One who lives in eternity. Because I don't understand everything about You, please make me wise. Help me learn something awesome today. Amen.

The LORD has told you what is good, and this is what he requires
of you: to do what is right, to love mercy,
and to walk humbly with your God.
MICAH 6:8 NLT

Dear God, You've given me three requirements that should be
priorities in my life. You want me to do the right thing. You want
me to be compassionate. You want me to respectfully follow where
You lead. Each of these priorities means that I do what You ask,
and You will always ask me to care for other people. If I follow You,
I will find people who need compassion. In those moments please
help me do the right thing. Your Word tells me this is good, and I
believe it is. Amen.

Whoever pursues righteousness and unfailing love
will find life, righteousness, and honor.
PROVERBS 21:21 NLT

Dear God, You've sent me on a journey, but instead of a pot of gold
at the end of a rainbow, You offer three gifts: life, righteousness,
and honor. To find these three gifts, I need to chase after
righteousness and unfailing love. The only place I find those
things is in You. Help me build endurance so I can be patient in
my journey. Help me build obedience so I can bring You honor.
Help me love You so I can really understand the life You want for
me. I can't do any of these things without Your help. Amen.

Jesus replied, " 'You must love the LORD your God
with all your heart, all your soul, and all your mind.'
This is the first and greatest commandment."
MATTHEW 22:37–38 NLT

Dear God, You've told me to love You, which sounds
easy. After all, You are the Creator of all cool stuff.
I can't go anywhere without seeing Your creativity.
Why is it easy to appreciate what You've made
and forget to appreciate You? If I'm supposed to
love You, then I need to know You. That means
more than understanding that You create sunsets,
crickets, and ocean waves. If I'm supposed to
love You with all my heart, soul, and mind, then
help me look beyond what You've created and
discover. . .You. Your Word always has the answers.
Thanks. Amen.

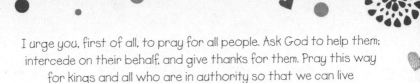

I urge you, first of all, to pray for all people. Ask God to help them;
intercede on their behalf, and give thanks for them. Pray this way
for kings and all who are in authority so that we can live
peaceful and quiet lives marked by godliness and dignity.
1 TIMOTHY 2:1–2 NLT

Dear God, You want me to prioritize the privilege of prayer. Some
of the prayers You want me to pray are for others. I should pray for
the wisdom I need, and when I do, I will understand that I can help
others by asking You to help them. I can thank You for the people
You introduce me to. I can pray for wisdom for leaders who have
hard decisions to make. When I'm unselfish in how I pray, then
You have the opportunity to respond to my prayers. Thanks for the
priority of unselfish prayer. Amen.

Pursue righteous living, faithfulness, love, and peace.
Enjoy the companionship of those who
call on the Lord with pure hearts.
2 TIMOTHY 2:22 NLT

Dear God, You want me to know I'm not alone in following Your
directions for my life. Your Word says that living in a way that
brings honor to You, being loyal to You, giving and receiving
Your love, and living peacefully with others are all priorities.
More than just priorities, these traits help me want to be with
other Christians who also follow You. When these priorities are
important to me, I will begin to see that I'm not the only one who
wants to live differently—for You. Amen.

> "Don't store up treasures here on earth, where moths eat them and rust destroys them, and where thieves break in and steal. Store your treasures in heaven, where moths and rust cannot destroy, and thieves do not break in and steal."
> MATTHEW 6:19-20 NLT

Dear God, You want decisions about my future to be a priority. Nothing seems to last forever. Trees die, riverbanks erode, and things that are really valuable sometimes get stolen. Your Word says that my greatest treasures are in heaven and they're completely safe. They won't be destroyed, and nobody can steal them. My treasures there are different than here. Instead of money or collections, my treasure is You and all the changes You've made in my family, my friends, and me. These are the treasures I want to see in heaven. Amen.

> Let us offer through Jesus a continual sacrifice of praise to God, proclaiming our allegiance to his name.
> HEBREWS 13:15 NLT

Dear God, You have made honor a powerful priority. Your Word says I am to honor my parents and those who are in charge, like teachers, Sunday school leaders, police officers, and the leaders of our country. More than honoring people around me, You want me to honor You most. I want to follow Your path for the rest of my life. No one is greater than You, and I am in awe that I get to be Your child. You are worthy of praise, and I'm just getting started. Amen.

Let us come boldly to the throne of our gracious God.
There we will receive his mercy, and we will find grace
to help us when we need it most.
HEBREWS 4:16 NLT

Dear God, You want me to know You are approachable. This can be hard to understand. You are so awesome, and there is no one like You. There will never be another like You. I'm amazed that You invite me to come to You even when I sin. You promise to forgive me when I don't deserve it, and offer me something better even though I didn't earn it. You call these two gifts mercy and grace. Your Word says these are things I will need, and I have needed them often. Thanks for being approachable. Amen.

[Jesus said,] "I am giving you a new commandment: Love each other.
Just as I have loved you, you should love each other. Your love for
one another will prove to the world that you are my disciples."
JOHN 13:34–35 NLT

Dear God, You say that being an example of Your love should be a priority for me. I know that loving You is important, but loving others can be harder because they aren't perfect. Maybe that's one of the lessons of love. A person doesn't have to be perfect to need or give love. If everyone waited for other people to be perfect to love them, then there wouldn't be much compassion. I will make loving others a priority. My love may not be perfect, but it will flow from my desire to obey You with all my heart. Amen.

Don't worry about anything; instead, pray about everything.
Tell God what you need, and thank him for all he has done.
Then you will experience God's peace, which exceeds anything
we can understand. His peace will guard your hearts
and minds as you live in Christ Jesus.
PHILIPPIANS 4:6-7 NLT

Dear God, You created the priority of contentment. To be content means I'm happy with what I have. When I'm content, I have peace. When I'm not content, I worry. Worry makes me ask a lot of "what-if" questions. What if things get harder? What if I look foolish when I sing in choir? What if I don't catch the ball? Contentment helps me enjoy living because I already know You love me in hard times, when I struggle to sing, and when I can't catch a ball. Still, You accept me. Amen.

MY WORLD—
THE POWER OF COMPASSION

If you want to show compassion, just do what Jesus did. It's easy to understand. Jesus fed people who were hungry, gave water to people who were thirsty, prayed for the hurting, and stood up for those who needed a friend. Showing compassion can be easy if you really like to help others, but it will need to be a choice if you struggle with serving others.

If you show compassion, you're giving something you don't expect to be returned. You choose kindness even when others are unkind. You make the decision to be thoughtful when others are not. You're gentle even when someone makes fun of you.

If you continually show compassion when others are unkind, they will begin to see there's more power in your compassion than in their rudeness. It's hard to dislike someone who really cares about you. If you want to see what compassion looks like, just look in the Bible. Compassion started with God. He remains compassionate even when we fail the kindness test.

All praise to God, the Father of our Lord Jesus Christ. God is our merciful Father and the source of all comfort. He comforts us in all our troubles so that we can comfort others. When they are troubled, we will be able to give them the same comfort God has given us.

2 CORINTHIANS 1:3–4 NLT

Dear God, You are a perfect example of compassion. You comfort me when I'm scared and help me when I need support. You know I need compassion. You also know I need to see what Your compassion looks like because You want me to show it to other people. You are the example I need to do what You ask me to do. You never leave me guessing what it looks like to choose Your way. I just need to spend time reading Your Word so I know what You have said in order to do what You ask. Amen.

Share each other's burdens,
and in this way obey the law of Christ.
GALATIANS 6:2 NLT

Dear God, You want me to share, but not always the way I think.
I know You want me to share what I have. I know You want me to
share my time with others. Your Word says I should share the things
that make other people sad. I know I should share the things that
are mine, but sharing something that belongs to someone else can
only mean that they don't know they need to share it. When I help
others endure the hard things they face, I move a little closer to true
compassion. Help me share. Amen.

•   •   •   •   •   •   •   •

So now there is no condemnation for those
who belong to Christ Jesus.
ROMANS 8:1 NLT

Dear God, Your compassion is a gift to those who believe in You.
Compassion can mean helping someone when they need help,
but it can also mean forgiving someone when they could be
condemned for—or found guilty of—breaking Your law. When I
believed that Jesus was Your Son and that when He died on the
cross He was the perfect sacrifice to pay the price for breaking
Your law, then You offered me compassion. I am no longer guilty
because Jesus set me free from sin's payment. Help me offer my
obedience in return. Amen.

The faithful love of the LORD never ends! His mercies never cease.
Great is his faithfulness; his mercies begin afresh each morning.
LAMENTATIONS 3:22–23 NLT

Dear God, Your compassion never expires. Your love never ends. Your mercies extend beyond the horizon. You cover me with a blanket of protection, shielding me from the harsh conditions I face. I will deal with problems. In fact, Your Word tells me I am guaranteed to have trouble, but You walk with me. You show Your love before, during, and after I face a challenge. I never have to handle hurt alone. You are always with me showing love that never changes and never goes away. Help me stay close to that compassionate love. Amen.

You, O Lord, are a God of compassion and mercy,
slow to get angry and filled with unfailing love and faithfulness.
PSALM 86:15 NLT

Dear God, You'd rather forgive then get angry. That's different from the way I sometimes feel. For me it's easier to get angry first and then think about whether I want to forgive the person who made me mad. When I think about it, I always like the feeling I get when anger goes away. If I forgive first, then I don't have to live through the frustration of being mad. You choose mercy. You decide on compassion. You hand out love more easily than free samples at the store. That's why You're God, and that's why I follow You. Amen.

Love each other with genuine affection,
and take delight in honoring each other.
ROMANS 12:10 NLT

Dear God, You want me to really love people, not just act like I do. If anybody knows the difference, it's You. Sometimes when I want to win, it can be hard to congratulate the actual winner, yet that's what You want. More than just a change in choice, You want to change my heart so I can really love and honor people. When I think I'm the only one who should win, I'm not really showing compassion for others. I should always do my best, but always rejoice with those who need it. Keep working on me. Amen.

Love is patient and kind. Love is not jealous
or boastful or proud.
1 CORINTHIANS 13:4 NLT

Dear God, Your Word tells me what love is, and it's not a feeling. Compassionate love is willing to wait, it trusts, and it is modest and humble. I know there's more to love than this, but I can decide to wait. I can trust and be modest. It's a decision You can help me with. Because You love me, help me follow. Amen.

Let all that I am praise the LORD; may I never forget the good things he does for me. He forgives all my sins and heals all my diseases. He redeems me from death and crowns me with love and tender mercies.
PSALM 103:2–4 NLT

Dear God, Your compassion changes something inside me. When I want to thank You, all I have to do is think back about all the things You've done for me. You created this world, my family, friends, joy, peace, and love. You give me life, forgive my sin, heal my hurts, and shower me with love and mercy. You do all this—for me. Whenever I need to understand why compassion is important, I just need to remember You, and I can't help but give You praise. You're amazing, God. Amen.

People who conceal their sins will not prosper, but if they confess
and turn from them, they will receive mercy.
PROVERBS 28:13 NLT

Dear God, You want my heart to be clean. I can't clean it myself, which is why You want me to be honest about what I've done. You want to hear about the good things. You want to show compassion in my struggles. My sins are also important to You. It isn't because You want to punish me, but because You want to remove my sin so I can get back to growing up. You want my permission to clean my heart, so help me share the good, the bad, and the ugly parts of my life with You. Thanks for forgiveness. Amen.

Kind words are like honey—sweet to the soul
and healthy for the body.
PROVERBS 16:24 NLT

Dear God, You really understand people. You know I like it when people are kind. Your Word says that if kindness were food, then it would be the sweetest thing around. Even though it's sweet, it's still healthy for me. Sometimes things that are good for me don't taste great, so this truth is awesome. Your Word even says that speaking kind words is healthy for the body. Maybe it's healthy because when I struggle with people, I don't feel good. More people should know about the healthy sweetness of being kind. Help me spread the word. Amen.

A gentle answer deflects anger,
but harsh words make tempers flare.
PROVERBS 15:1 NLT

Dear God, there are some things You don't want me to do if my goal is to be compassionate. I've been motivated to be kind to others because You've been a perfect role model. But Your Word tells me that everyone can make bad choices when they are angry. You say I can help others avoid being angry by using compassionate responses even when being angry would be easier. If anger is like a wildfire, then please use the way I respond to help put out the flames. Amen.

Encourage each other and build each other up,
just as you are already doing.
1 THESSALONIANS 5:11 NLT

Dear God, You want to use me to encourage other people. It's easy to feel as if my best is never good enough. All the decorating I can do to a kiddie pool doesn't change the fact it's just a kiddie pool. I've seen what You've done with a lake. Now that's impressive. When I feel like a failure, it's easy to believe that other people sometimes feel that way, too. You want me to help my family, friends, and neighbors see that they can always do more when they accept Your help. I want to be that kind of encouragement. Amen.

> Your kindness will reward you,
> but your cruelty will destroy you.
> PROVERBS 11:17 NLT

Dear God, You tell me I'll be rewarded for being kind. You say that being mean will crush me. Since no one has given me a kindness award and I haven't been destroyed for being mean, You must have a different way for me to understand Your words. Showing compassion helps others, and it helps me. Being cruel hurts others, and it hurts me. Even if I have to wait, I'm always better off when I choose Your guidance over how I feel. Being mean makes my heart and mind twisted and ugly. Help me remember the true rewards of compassion. Amen.

> Whenever we have the opportunity, we should do good to
> everyone—especially to those in the family of faith.
> GALATIANS 6:10 NLT

Dear God, You want my life to be a billboard for compassion. You want my heart to give gentleness a leadership role. You want me to go into business with kindness. You say that caring for others is an opportunity. Being like Jesus is hard because I have sinned and I'm not perfect. Help me pay attention to those times when You give me an opportunity to show compassion to others. Help me do what I know You'd want. Amen.

Oh, the joys of those who are kind to the poor!
The LORD rescues them when they are in trouble.
The LORD protects them and keeps them alive.
PSALM 41:1–2 NLT

Dear God, You want me to be kind to people who struggle. You are kind to me, and I struggle. Now I get it. You always want me to do what You do. You love me, so I should love others. You show me mercy, so I should do the same thing. You rescue people in trouble, and You rescued me when I was in trouble. Sometimes I make things harder than I should. You don't ask me to do something You haven't already done. When I do what You do, You promise the gift of joy. Thanks, God. Amen.

MY WORRY—
THE POWER OF PEACE

Have you ever wondered why you worry?

You might think worrying over a problem will help the problem go away, but it just wastes time and energy on something you can't change or control. You may know that God understands all things and wants to develop a plan for a good outcome, but you struggle with anxiety. When you worry, you act as if God is too small to take care of the things He actually controls.

The worry you decide to think about may be yours, but God wants to take it from you and replace it with peace. When your mind and heart are peaceful, there's not much room for worry. On the other hand, when your heart and mind are worried, there's not much room for peace.

Let God take the things you worry about. It's not a burden for Him. He already knows how the story ends. Maybe that's why He's not worried, and you shouldn't be either.

For peace to grow, show worry the door.

Be still in the presence of the LORD, and wait patiently
for him to act. Don't worry about evil people who
prosper or fret about their wicked schemes.
PSALM 37:7 NLT

Dear God, You need me to be patient while I wait
for Your answers. Sometimes I worry so much about
whether You'll answer, how You'll answer, and when
the answer will come. This happens especially when
I think about other people who seem to be rewarded
for doing the wrong thing. When I notice myself
worrying about the bad decisions other people
make, You ask me to stop and wait patiently, and at
the right time You will take care of things. Thanks,
Lord. Amen.

Give all your worries and cares to God,
for he cares about you.
1 PETER 5:7 NLT

Dear God, You want me to give You the worst possible gift, and getting rid of it is for my own good. Worries are things I hang on to because I think really bad stuff will happen. My mind can take off in a dozen directions so I can't sleep or concentrate, and my joy goes into hibernation. Your Word says You care about me and You can take care of any worry that introduces itself to me. It doesn't seem like the greatest gift, but since You want it, help me give worry a new home with You. Amen.

"Can all your worries add a single moment to your life?"
MATTHEW 6:27 NLT

Dear God, You have a question, and You want an answer. Can worry make me live longer? The answer is no. Worry has taken time away from really living because instead of spending moments with people I love, I spend them worrying about things I can't control. Why do I do that? Right now it doesn't make sense to hold on to worry, but I will probably worry again, and each second I refuse to let You handle things is another second I will struggle with trust. Help me remember You are faithful to take care of me. Amen.

Worry weighs a person down;
an encouraging word cheers a person up.
PROVERBS 12:25 NLT

Dear God, You send people to help me remember who You are.
These friends are like a life vest for someone who can't swim very
well. They help keep my head above water because they share
helpful words when I'm weary from worry. These are good friends
to have, and it's the kind of friend I want to be. You created each of
us to be able to give gifts of encouraging words. Each of us needs
support. Help me trust You and encourage others to give trust a
try. Amen.

Then Jesus said, "Come to me, all of you who are weary
and carry heavy burdens, and I will give you rest."
MATTHEW 11:28 NLT

Dear God, You want me to get a good night's rest. Sometimes I
wake up in the middle of the night and I'm worried about a lot of
stuff. It could be whether the front door is locked or if I did all my
homework. I roll around like a rotisserie chicken. I don't get any
rest. I'm usually grouchy in the morning. I worry about big things,
small things, and some in the middle of the worry scale. Because
I'm weary, You ask me to bring my sack of assorted burdens to
You. That sounds really good. I'm tired. Amen.

[Jesus said,] "I am leaving you with a gift—peace of mind and heart.
And the peace I give is a gift the world cannot give.
So don't be troubled or afraid."
JOHN 14:27 NLT

Dear God, when it comes to worry, Your Word says it should be avoided, never purchased, and if I have any worry lying around, I should let You take it. Your replacement gift is peace, which is different than thinking of a world that doesn't need soldiers. Your peace is being confident You can take care of anything I could possibly worry about. Life can be hard, but Your peace means no matter how bad things get, I don't need to be afraid because You're big enough to manage all the worry in the world. Amen.

[Jesus said,] "Don't let your hearts be troubled.
Trust in God, and trust also in me."
JOHN 14:1 NLT

Dear God, how did You know I have trouble trusting? Well, I suppose it's because You're God and You know everything. Since You know everything, it makes sense that Your Word tells me to never allow my heart to become worried. When I worry, I find it hard to believe that anyone can handle what I go through except me. Then again, I never really handle things well when I worry, and I either forget or refuse to let You handle my troubles. Remind me often that I need to trust You. Amen.

When I am afraid, I will put my trust in you.
I praise God for what he has promised.
I trust in God, so why should I be afraid?
PSALM 56:3–4 NLT

Dear God, Your promises make trusting You much easier. Every time I'm afraid of all the things that might happen, You want me to think of all the things You have promised. You want me to see that Your Word is filled with promises that have already been kept. You have always been worth trusting. You've always taken care of those who follow You. Help me remember the things You have done, and then help me to remember to say thanks. Worry and fear can't compare to trust and praise. Keep reminding me of Your promises. Amen.

When doubts filled my mind,
your comfort gave me renewed hope and cheer.
PSALM 94:19 NLT

Dear God, You bring the deepest comfort, the greatest hope, and the most joyous cheer I need when doubt drops by with friends. Sometimes I try to be brave and confident. I try to convince myself and other people that I never have doubts, but I think I do a very bad job of being confident. I can doubt that my friends like me, that I'm ready for a test, or that I will ever be good at anything. I need Your comfort, hope, and cheer. Let me never doubt Your love. Amen.

Give your burdens to the LORD, and he will take care of you.
He will not permit the godly to slip and fall.
PSALM 55:22 NLT

Dear God, You want my "worry backpack" to be empty. I know I don't really have a worry backpack, but it can seem like it. The more worry I carry, the heavier it seems to get. The heavier it is, the harder it is for me to find joy. The harder it is to find joy, the sadder I become. The sadder I am, the harder it is to follow You. If I worry less, then I can follow You more. When You take care of me, I can enjoy walking with You. Help me walk without worry. Amen.

> May the Lord of peace himself give you his peace
> at all times and in every situation.
> 2 THESSALONIANS 3:16 NLT

Dear God, Your Word calls You the Lord of peace. This special name helps me understand that You want peace to overflow in my life like a waterfall. You want me to accept Your peace in every situation I face. Help me stay away from drama that distracts me from Your peace. Help me encourage others to accept Your peace. Help me love Your peace enough to accept it instead of hugging the hurtful choice of worry. Help me find a home within Your peace so when bad days come my heart is at home with You. Amen.

> [Jesus said,] "Here on earth you will have many trials and sorrows.
> But take heart, because I have overcome the world."
> JOHN 16:33 NLT

Dear God, if life is a battle between good and evil, You win. I would love to live in a world where life is easy, people are kind, and bad things just don't happen to good people. I don't live in this kind of world. Since each person gets to make choices, I might get sad because some of their decisions will make things difficult for me. When worry comes knocking, I can send him away without inviting him in because You have overcome the power of sinful choices. Thanks for being my defender. Amen.

In peace I will lie down and sleep, for you alone,
O Lord, will keep me safe.
Psalm 4:8 NLT

Dear God, You work the night shift so I can sleep in peace. You don't need sleep, but I do. When I lie down to sleep, help me remember that You watch over me. You want the best for me, and the absolute best gift when I need to sleep is peace. Your gifts make me thankful. Amen.

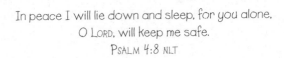

Look at those who are honest and good,
for a wonderful future awaits those who love peace.
Psalm 37:37 NLT

Dear God, You want me to chase after peace because Your Word says that "a wonderful future awaits those who love peace." Even if there weren't a promise of a wonderful future, I'd love Your peace more than my chaos. To have peace means worry can't find a place to rest in my heart. To have peace means my face shows joy more than fear. To have peace means anger is less likely to come between friendships. I love Your peace. Help me keep it as a permanent change in the way I live and in the way I respond to others. Amen.

Those who trust in the LORD will find new strength.
They will soar high on wings like eagles. They will run
and not grow weary. They will walk and not faint.
ISAIAH 40:31 NLT

Dear God, Your Word tells me how I can be strong. You want my life to demonstrate that I can endure difficult times. My strength comes from You. I grow stronger when I trust, and weaker when I worry. Your Word says I can move forward without worry and without being exhausted. Help me make the brave choice to trust You with every worry. I don't have to wonder whether You're the right One to handle any trouble. The minute I spot worry, let me run to You—and drop it off. Amen.

SCRIPTURE INDEX

OLD TESTAMENT

Genesis
2:2. . .147
2:7. . .27
2:18. . .127
18:13–14. . .96

Exodus
4:10. . .107
15:2. . .175
15:12. . .177
15:20. . .107
20:3. . .192
20:12. . .61

Deuteronomy
6:2. . .67

Joshua
1:9. . .172
24:15. . .62

1 Samuel
16:7. . .21
20:17. . .87
30:6. . .172

1 Chronicles
16:11. . .42, 175

Job
10:12. . .27
23:12. . .33

Psalms
1:1–2. . .34
1:2. . .143
4:8. . .145, 217
18:32–34. . .178
25:4. . .166
25:5. . .166
27:1. . .171, 174
31:24. . .176
32:8. . .164
37:7. . .210
37:24. . .41
37:37. . .217
39:7. . .55
41:1–2. . .208
41:9. . .84
55:22. . .215
56:3–4. . .214
62:5. . .52
71:5. . .56
86:15. . .202
90:12. . .192
94:11. . .95
94:19. . .57, 215
103:2–4. . .204
119:8. . .31
119:9. . .165

119:11...37
119:15...167
119:23...173
119:63...86
119:105...141
138:8...95
139:14...21
139:16...97
147:10–11...25

Proverbs
1:5...160
1:7...168
1:8...62
2:8...77
2:11...118
3:3...70
3:5...114
3:5–6...42, 54
3:6...114
4:13...161
9:9...163
9:10...165
10:14...162
10:28...51
11:16...127
11:17...207
11:29...61
12:25...212
13:1...112
15:1...121, 206
15:13...23
16:16...162

16:18...12
16:24...205
16:28...82
17:9...82
17:17...88
17:22...12
18:15...163
18:24...83
19:20...161
21:21...193
22:24–25...126
23:18...56
23:24–25...15
25:28...181
27:6...83
27:9...86
27:17...85
28:7...85
28:13...205
29:15...63
31:20...122
31:25...97
31:26...125
31:30...22

Ecclesiastes
3:11...93
3:15...91
5:7...53

Isaiah
30:21...58
40:8...36

40:31. . .218
41:10. . .176
53:2–3. . .24
55:8–9. . .93
55:11. . .30
66:2. . .123

Jeremiah
1:4–5. . .108
29:11. . .51, 91
33:3. . .53

Lamentations
3:22–23. . .202
3:24. . .55

Daniel
1:17. . .106

Micah
6:8. . .193

Zephaniah
3:17. . .128

NEW TESTAMENT

Matthew
1:16. . .67
4:4. . .31
5:16. . .105
5:47. . .80

6:2. . .25
6:5. . .148
6:6. . .147
6:7. . .143
6:9. . .142
6:19–20. . .196
6:27. . .211
6:33. . .191
7:3. . .81
8:2. . .108
11:28. . .212
14:23. . .145
20:27–28. . .103
22:37–38. . .194
23:28. . .26
24:35. . .33
26:39. . .144

Mark
12:31. . .65

Luke
7:50. . .71
8:24–25. . .78
10:33–34. . .104
10:39–42. . .68
12:7. . .23
12:34. . .57, 191
19:10. . .156
21:19. . .43

John
1:1. . .32

1:12...137
3:16...155
8:34...110
9:10-11...96
10:27...35
12:26...105
13:23...87
13:34-35...197
14:1...213
14:6...156
14:27...47, 213
15:9...133
15:15...136
16:33...124, 216
17:17...35

Acts
4:12...153
22:14-16...94

Romans
1:12...75
3:22...75
4:5...76
5:2...76
5:3-5...48
5:10...81
6:23...112
8:1...201
8:26...146
8:28...92
8:29...135
8:37-39...98

10:9...157
10:13...157
12:2...190
12:4-5...101
12:6-8...100
12:10...203
12:12...46
12:19...186
14:17-18...13
15:4...37, 131
15:5-6...11

1 Corinthians
1:27...177
2:5...71
6:19-20...26
9:24...182
9:25...182
10:13...44, 111
13:4...203
13:4-5...120
13:4-7...60
14:33...188
16:13...72

2 Corinthians
1:3-4...200
4:18...77
5:17...137
5:20...131
5:21...151
12:9-10...170

Galatians
1:10. . .123
2:16. . .158
2:20. . .74, 138
3:26. . .73
5:22–23. . .149
6:2. . .201
6:9. . .46, 113
6:10. . .63, 207

Ephesians
1:5. . .65
2:8. . .134
2:9. . .155
3:12. . .72
4:22–24. . .11
4:24. . .136
4:25. . .133
4:26. . .15
4:29. . .16
5:1. . .110
5:15. . .187
6:1. . .185
6:1–4. . .64
6:18. . .45

Philippians
1:6. . .130
2:22. . .103
2:5–7. . .10
2:14. . .121
2:14–15. . .14
3:20. . .135

4:6. . .52
4:6–7. . .198
4:8. . .40
4:13. . .117, 169, 173

Colossians
1:17. . .92
2:6. . .115, 153
3:1. . .130
3:12. . .132
3:14. . .122
3:17. . .116
3:23–24. . .106

1 Thessalonians
2:13. . .38
5:11. . .206
5:16–18. . .47
5:22. . .185

2 Thessalonians
3:16. . .216

1 Timothy
2:1–2. . .195
2:9–10. . .20
3:11. . .126
4:7. . .183
4:8. . .22
4:13. . .32
6:10. . .50

2 Timothy
1:7. . .171
2:22. . .195
3:14. . .115
3:16. . .142

Titus
2:2. . .183
2:12. . .181
3:2. . .125
3:4–5. . .150

Hebrews
4:12–13. . .18
4:16. . .197
6:10. . .102
11:1. . .74
13:5. . .16, 184
13:8. . .43
13:15. . .196

James
1:5. . .167
1:12. . .45
1:19. . .17, 186
2:17. . .73
3:12–13. . .90
3:18. . .187
5:13. . .141
5:16. . .140

1 Peter
3:3–4. . .28
3:8. . .13
3:18. . .154
4:9. . .102
4:10. . .101
5:7. . .41, 211

2 Peter
1:5–7. . .180
3:9. . .152

1 John
1:7. . .152
2:28. . .117
3:9. . .66
5:12. . .151

Jude
1:20–21. . .70